NEW FRANKENSTEINS

BLITZ EDITIONS

Published by Blitz Editions
an imprint of Bookmart Ltd
Registered Number 2372865
Trading as Bookmart Ltd
Desford Road
Enderby
Leicester LE9 5AD

ISBN 1 85605 213 3

This material has previously appeared in *Inside Stories.*

Every effort has been made to contact the copyright holders for the pictures. In some cases they have been untraceable, for which we offer our apologies. Special thanks to the Hulton-Deutsch Collection, who supplied the majority of pictures, and thanks also to the following libraries and picture agencies: Aerospace/Midsummer Books, Bilderdienst Suddeutscher Verlag, Peter Newark/Western Americana, Popperfotos, Rex Features, Frank Spooner, Syndication International, Topham Picture Source

This book was produced by Amazon Publishing Limited
Designed by Cooper Wilson Design
Edited by Graham McColl

Printed in the Slovak Republic
51726

NEW FRANKENSTEINS

JACK KEVORKIAN
Doctor Death

Jack Kevorkian is an American doctor who helps the terminally ill to die. His activities have caused great controversy in the US. Is he an angel of mercy or an angel of death? Is he an enlightened humanitarian or someone who, but for legal loopholes, would already be behind bars?

America knows him simply as 'Doctor Death'. But Jack Kevorkian, a 64-year-old retired physician, prefers to compare himself to that other misunderstood medical genius – Doctor Frankenstein. But where Frankenstein sought to give life, Kevorkian seeks to take it.

DOCTOR FRANKENSTEIN SOUGHT TO GIVE LIFE BUT DOCTOR KEVORKIAN, 'DOCTOR DEATH', SEEKS TO TAKE IT

Left: ***The creature Frankenstein as played by Boris Karloff. Kevorkian likes to compare himself to the mythical doctor who created the monster.***

Opposite: ***Dr Jack Kevorkian. To many he is a saint who relieves suffering. But the authorities have branded him a 'ghoul'.***

Below: ***The doctor with his 'suicide machine', which brings death to users within a minute.***

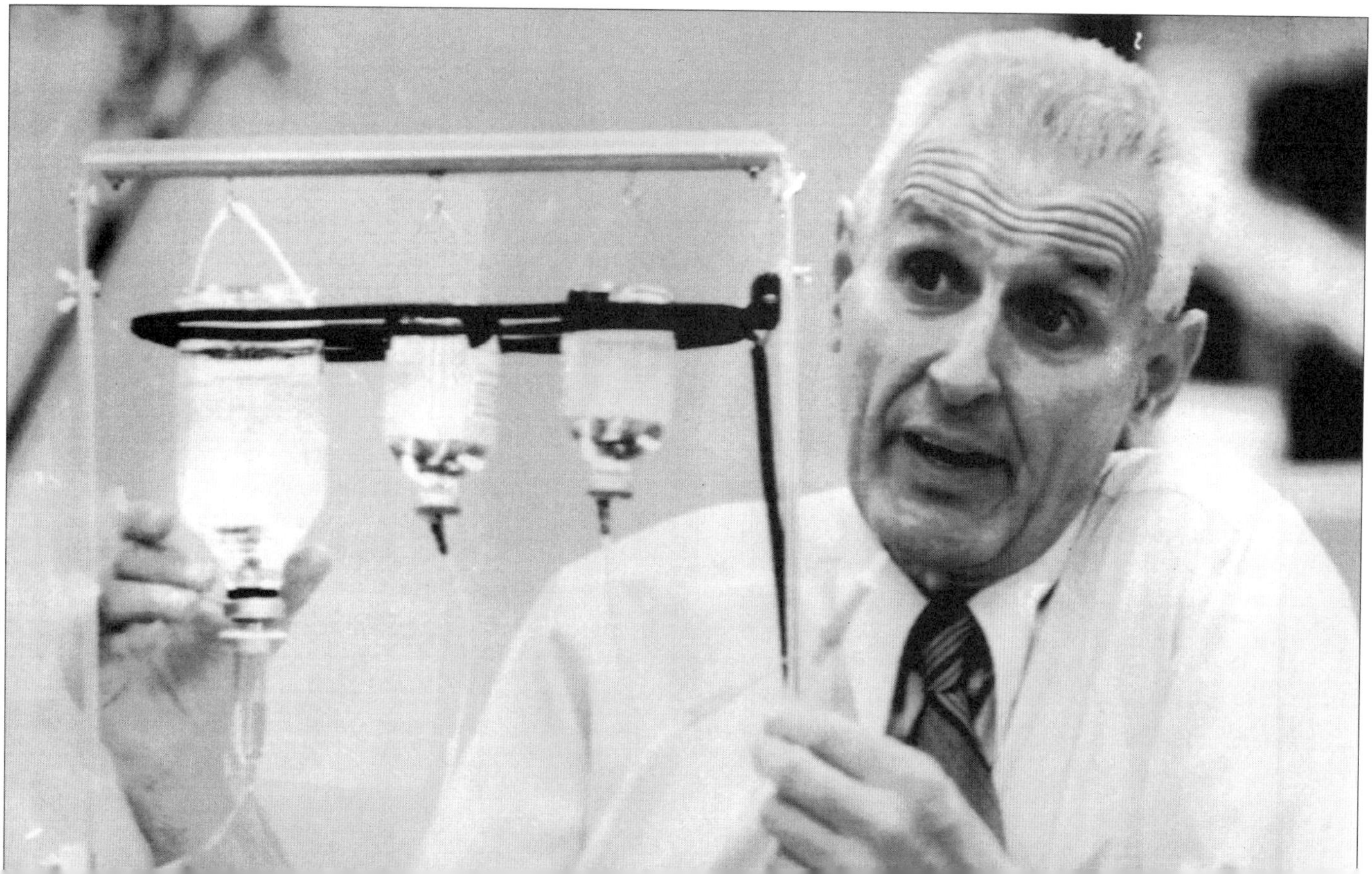

Above: ***A monster or a saint? Dr Kevorkian argues his point fiercely in court.***

Opposite Top: ***The van that police dubbed 'The Deathmobile'. Inside it Janet Adkins, 54, committed suicide, hooked up to his suicide machine. She was the first to die using it.***

Opposite Bottom: ***Janet Adkins and her husband Neil on their wedding day.***

With the aid of his controversial 'Suicide Machine', the former pathologist has already helped at least 16 chronically ill people take their own lives, and his avid belief in the individual's right to terminate one's own existence has fuelled a legal, ethical and medical debate across the entire country.

The device, made from salvaged parts he picked up here and there at flea markets and garage sales, intravenously feeds death-inducing drugs or poisonous gas to a patient, after the victim has pushed the machine's button. The white-haired doctor claims he is 'dedicated to the honourable and ethical practice of alleviating hopelessly irremediable physical suffering'. But his many critics claim he is trying to play God.

Kevorkian, who began practising medicine in 1952, has had a long – and many would also say morbid – fascination with death and other macabre subjects. In the mid-1950s, while working at the University of Michigan Medical Centre, he admits he 'used to take what I called death rounds. I would go around to all of the people (in the hospital) who were about to die and watch. I wanted to see at what point they could no longer be resuscitated. But I don't like to watch someone die. It is a traumatic, wrenching experience'.

THE EARLY PLAN

There was also his early plan, first proposed during his medical school days and shunned by his professors, to 'harvest' organs from prison inmates. There were experiments in how best to take blood from corpses, which he first learned about in 1961 from articles based on the Soviet practice in which blood from freshly-dead corpses was used for transfusions on the battlefield where no other bloody supply was handy. Kevorkian did his own experiments, taking 'blood from immediately dead people – from their heart through a special syringe – into the recipient'.

The practice did not gain popularity because, according to a magazine report of the time, 'US doctors have shied away from it because of prejudice against contact with anything from a corpse'.

Kevorkian, of course, disagreed, saying that blood was no different from an organ for transplant, and that 'superstition' had cost many lives. But his professional reputation was damaged by the controversy, and he admits that he found it hard to obtain work after that.

Later, the defiant doctor again raised eyebrows when he advocated giving death-row prisoners the right to commit suicide, with their organs removed while comatose, rather than be executed.

He said he got the idea from his days as a young resident in pathology, when he was dealing with death-row criminals who wanted to make a final gesture of penitence by donating their organs so that they might save a life. Again, the medical community was shocked. 'They told me you've got to drop the idea or leave the university. So I left the university', he recalled.

Above: ***Leslie Williams, 81, and wife Susan, 52. Susan chose to die with Kevorkian present at her end.***

Top: ***Kevorkian with Marcella Lawrence (left) and Marguerite Tate, who both took their life with 'Doctor Death' present.***

For many years, Kevorkian devoted himself to writing on death and euthanasia, and wrote many books which were just as controversial as his earlier ideas. But most of the leading medical journals and magazines in the US refused his articles, and Kevorkian slipped into relative anonymity within the medical fraternity. Certainly, his name was unfamiliar to the public. But that, of course, would change...and soon. In 1989, he first began tinkering with the so-called 'Suicide Machine', following a meeting with David Rivlin, who had become a quadriplegic in 1971 following a terrible surfing accident. In 1989, at the age of 38 and having spent half his life without the use of his limbs, he made up his mind that he wanted to die. But no one at the nursing home he lived in would help him so the desperate man made a public appeal to a Detroit newspaper, in which he begged a doctor to help him commit suicide. Only one doctor responded. It was Kevorkian, who stepped into the spotlight and offered to discuss it with him, but the courts immediately said no.

Still, Kevorkian continued tinkering with his machine and by September 1989 he had it ready to use. When a local medical journal refused to take an advertisement from him regarding its availability, a Detroit newspaper ran a story on him. The following year, he got his chance to use it when he performed his first medically-assisted suicide in June, with the death of a 54-year-old Alzheimer's sufferer from Oregon who travelled to Michigan to die. Janet Adkins had come to him in eagerness to end her life before the full ravages of the disease became unbearable. Kevorkian was ready for his first patient – in fact, he was so keen to realise his idea of medically-assisted suicide that he even had business cards printed. On them, he called himself an 'Obitiatrist', from the word 'obituary' – a doctor of death. 'The world's first', he adds quite proudly.

When Adkins, a mother of three, arrived, she climbed into the back of Kevorkian's old Volkswagen van in a rural Michigan park and watched as he connected her to his Suicide Machine. She then pushed a button three times to ensure the machine's death-inducing drugs would pour into her veins. Her last words, said Kevorkian, were: 'Thank you, thank you'. Her husband Ron, who was there when she died, said his wife 'was very happy to exit. She believed in Dr Kevorkian. She looked into his eyes and said "thank you."'

VIDEO EVIDENCE

Also, Adkins left behind a video-tape, which she apparently made just two days before she died. Adkins, a plump, bespectacled woman, is seen being interviewed by Kevorkian:

Q. Janet, are you are of you decision?
A. Yes.
Q. What does it mean?
A. You have to get out with dignity.
Q. Just what is it you want? Put it in simple English.
A. Self-deliverance.
Q. Do you want to go on?
A. No, I don't want to go on.
Q. What does that mean?
A. The end of...my life.
Q. What's the word for it?
A. Euthanasia.
Q. No, what's the word for the end of life?
A. You're dead.
Q. All right, is that what you wish?
A. Yes.

The next day, when the doctor spoke publicly of her death, the debate began. But if the medical community – and many ordinary citizens – were appalled at the thought of a doctor helping a patient to commit suicide, then Kevorkian was equally appalled at the reaction to his behaviour. 'The medical society is stuck in the Dark Ages', he said recently. 'I'm sure if they could, they would burn me at the stake'.

Above: ***Another controversy for Kevorkian, after he learns that he will not stand trial on murder charges.***

Not quite, but in March 1991 Kevorkian was charged with the murder of Adkins, but the case was later dismissed. A judge ruled that assisted suicide was not illegal in Michigan and therefore the doctor had committed no criminal act. However, the judge warned Kevorkian that he was not to assist in any more suicides. For a while, the doctor heeded that warning. But fifteen months later, he defied the order. Two more women, Sherry Miller, 43, and Marjorie Wantz, 58, killed themselves with the doctor's assistance. Miller, suffering from multiple sclerosis, took a lethal dose of carbon monoxide from a device which released the deadly gas through a mask placed over her head. Wantz, who had a painful pelvic dis-

ADKINS CLIMBED INTO KEVORKIAN'S VAN AND WATCHED HIM CONNECT HER TO HIS SUICIDE MACHINE

Above: ***Kevorkian with his attorney Geoffrey Fieger in 1991 after having assisted in the suicide of two people. He again escaped prosecution.***

'IT'S TOUGH TO FIND PROBABLE CAUSE FOR MURDER... THESE WOMEN COMMITTED SUICIDE. HE PROVIDED THE MEANS

A PROSECUTOR LABELLED KEVORKIAN 'JEFFREY DAHMER IN A LAB COAT', REFERRING TO THE KILLER WHO ATE 17 VICTIMS

ease, took a fatal injection of drugs administered by the machine. Both women died, side by side, in a secluded cabin in rural Michigan.

Before they died, both spoke on a videotape made by Kevorkian, and made plain their reasons for wanting to end their suffering. 'People tell me you should get out and do this, hang in there', said Miller. 'But you're in such misery that you can't wait to pop a sleeping pill and go to bed, just to get out of the pain'.

Again, murder charges were filed against Kevorkian. District Court Judge James Sheehy, while acknowledging the absence of a law preventing the doctor from assisting in suicides, said some serious questions had been raised in the deaths of Wantz and Miller. Although both women had painful ailments neither was considered terminally ill.

PROBABLE CAUSE FOR MURDER

Despite the medical community's antagonism towards Kevorkian, the Hemlock Society, an Oregon-based association which supports doctor-assisted suicides, said it was shocked that he would be tried in the deaths. 'I had expected they would drop those murder charges', said Hemlock attorney Cheryl Smith. 'I think that it's tough to find probable cause for murder because these women committed suicide. He provided the means'.

But prosecutors believed Wantz and Miller were incapable of making a rational decision. 'Wantz was mentally ill', said state attorney Lawrence Bunting. 'There was nothing wrong with this lady except she needed mental health treatment and now she's dead because Kevorkian decided to take the law into his own hands. People like Kevorkian can do all sorts of damage'.

'What he did is like veterinary medicine', added Dr John Finn, medical director of a Detroit hospital where some terminally ill patients have tried to seek out Kevorkian's services. 'When you take your pet to the vet, he puts the pet to sleep. I think human beings are more complicated than that'.

One local prosecutor, Richard Thompson of Oakland County, Michigan went so far as to label Kevorkian as 'Jeffrey Dahmer in a lab coat', referring to the monstrous serial killer who murdered and ate 17 boys and young men in Milwaukee.

Yet despite all the outrage, none of the charges ever stuck, because Kevorkian had only assisted in the suicides, and had never done the deed himself. So he was again free to carry out his mission as Doctor Death, caring not a fig for the growing furore. However, authorities revoked his medical licence, which cut off his supply of the death-inducing drugs he needed, so he switched to using carbon monoxide. 'We were told in medical school that carbon monoxide was the best way to commit suicide', he told an interviewer, not seeming to care that he could no longer obtain drugs for his work. 'All you do is get a tank of gas and a mask to breathe it through. The gas offers a simple, painless, odourless death. Better than that, it leaves the corpse looking good. You look better dead than alive. Gives your corpse a lovely, rosy glow'.

In all, Kevorkian has now helped a total of 16 people – ten within the past 12 months prior to July 1993 – kill themselves. Among them: Susan Williams, 52, who wrote 'I'm happy to have his assistance, since I am unable to do this myself', suffered from multiple sclerosis. Lois Hawes, 52, who had lung cancer; Catherine Andreyev, 46, cancer; Marcella Lawrence, 67, heart disease, who once said 'I wish (the law-makers) could have my pain for one night'; Marguerite Tate, 70, Lou Gehrig's disease; Jack Miller, 53, the first male, who had bone cancer. The list continues (the most recent came in May 1993).

'CARBON MONOXIDE LEAVES THE CORPSE LOOKING GOOD, IT GIVES YOUR CORPSE A LOVELY, ROSY GLOW'

DEFIANT DOCTOR

The defiant doctor helped seven of those commit suicide just before a law banning doctor-assisted suicide went into effect in March 1993. 'I don't care about the law', he said. 'I have never cared about anything but the welfare of the patient in front of me. I help people when their time comes. I haven't killed anybody. I haven't abused this, it's legal'.

Indeed, that Michigan law banning assisted-suicide faced an immediate challenge. The American Civil Liberties Union (ACLU) filed suit against the ban on the grounds that the decision to end one's own

Below: ***Fieger staves off reporters and Kevorkian manages a smile after being bailed from a police station on a charge of assisting in a suicide.***

life is an individual right and protected by the US constitution. 'The state has no business dictating an intensely private decision', the ACLU argued. In May 1993, an appeals court agreed, and struck down the law, concluding: 'This court cannot envisage a more fundamental right than the right to self-determination.'

One of the assisted suicides Kevorkian conducted just prior to the law's inception was that of Hugh Gale, a 70-year-old with emphysema and heart disease, who died in his living room with his wife by his side after breathing carbon monoxide. Right-to-life advocates claim they found a document in the garbage that may have indicated that Gale changed his mind at the last minute and wanted desperately to live.

ANOTHER DEATH

The document, called a Final Action Form, and reportedly signed by Kevorkian, claims that Gale asked that the mask be taken off after less than one minute, but then changed his mind again and asked that the gas be continued. After about 20 minutes, with nasal oxygen continuing, the mask was replaced over his nose and mouth, and he again pulled the clip off the crimped tubing. 'In about 30-35 seconds, he again flushed, became agitated with moderate hyperpnea (rapid or deep breathing) and immediately after saying "Take it off!" once again, he fell into unconsciousness. The mask was then left in place...Heartbeat was undetectable about three minutes after last breath'.

Originally, Prosecutor Carl Marlinga said if the document proved authentic, it suggested that death was involuntary and that at the last minute the patient changed his mind,' and charges would be filed against Kevorkian. But Gale's wife, Cheryl, says her husband did not want to stop the suicide process, as did their son, Hugh Jnr., who praised Kevorkian. 'He's really gone out on a limb and look what he's going through', said Hugh. 'Either he's a raving lunatic or he's very strongly committed to helping people. I'm thankful my dad's suffering was finally ended'. Kevorkian's attorney, Geoffrey Fieger, angrily claimed the document had been faked by right-to-life activists who staunchly oppose the doctor's work. 'At some point you got to stop responding to this lunacy', said Fieger. 'A bunch of right-wing Christian nuts again called Dr Kevorkian a murderer. It's laughable'. Eventually, the prosecutor declined to press murder charges.

Above: ***Publicity-hound Kevorkian gets a last-minute once-over before he goes on air in Detroit.***

KEVORKIAN KNOWS FIRST HAND THE TRAGEDY OF WATCHING A LOVED ONE WASTE AWAY FROM A DEBILITATING DISEASE

Kevorkian, a tart-tongued, grey-haired man of 64, who grew up in Pontiac, Michigan, knows first hand the tragedy of watching a loved one waste away from a debilitating disease. 'Our mother suffered from cancer', said his sister, Margo Janus. 'I saw the ravages right up to the end. Her mind was sound, but her body was gone. My brother's option would have been more moral than all the Demerol (pain killers) that they poured into her, to the point that her body was all black and blue from the needle marks. She was in a coma, and she weighed only 70 pounds. Even then I said to the doctor, "This isn't right, to keep her on I.V.", but he shrugged his shoulder and said, "I'm bound by my oath to do that".'

Who knows what effect that horrible experience had on the young Kevorkian, but it is known that while he was studying at the University of Michigan Medical School, his morbid fascination with pathology first came to the fore. He was engrossed with the history of autopsies, and says the ancient Greeks performed assisted suicides thousands of years ago. When he became a doctor, he says he didn't set out to be a medical heretic, but one night that all changed when he was doing his late-night rounds. I was making rounds one night and there was this woman who was dying of liver cancer', he recalled many years later. 'It was horrible, her belly was swollen up so much her skin was almost transparent, you could see the veins. She was in horrible, intractable pain. It looked like she was pleading for death with her eyes. But we couldn't give her that. We had to keep her going, prolonging the agony. It was cruel and barbaric'.

Given the long history of assisted suicide in ancient cultures, Kevorkian says 'I'm not early, I'm late'. And he claims that in the not too distant future 'medicide' as he calls it will be legal. 'You cannot fight changing mores'.

Indeed, this is already happening to some extent in the United States, and Kevorkian has found allies within the growing right-to-die movement, which is being fanned by America's mounting opposition to technology that extends lives regardless of the pain involved for the patient, or the suffering for the family. 'If we are free people at all, then we must be free to choose the manner of our death', said Derek Humphry, Executive Director of the Hemlock Society. But even Humphry agrees with euthanasia opponents when he says Kevorkian is not the right man for the job. 'He's a strange bird', he said. 'A zealot' Indeed, during the hearing into Adkins' death, Kevorkian acted as his own lawyer and his frequent arrogant outbursts – including numerous swear words – supported those who insist the doctor isn't the right man to play God.

THE GHOUL'S SIDE OF THE STORY

Kevorkian, who says he gets about 200 letters a year from people asking him to help them die, says he is not a ghoul, but a man who is devoted to ending suffering. 'These are not happy moments', he said. 'The ending of a human life can never be a good moment. I will help a suffering human being at the right time when the patient's

Below: ***The front page of the* New York Post *after the grim reaper claims another human being.***

AUTO SATURDAY

Special car buyer's bonanza inside

FOUNDED IN 1801 BY ALEXANDER HAMILTON

NEW YORK POST

SPORTS EXTRA

SATURDAY, MAY 16/SUNDAY, MAY 17, 1992 / Rain, mid 60s today; cloudy, mid 50s tonight / Details, Page 2

40¢ in New York City 50¢ elsewhere

Another patient kills self with Kevorkian's 'advice'

DR. DEATH AT IT AGAIN

Jack Kevorkian, the "Suicide Doc," did not assist in the "self-administered carbon monoxide" death of a woman yesterday, his lawyer said. PAGE 4

Associated Press

ALEXANDER'S CLOSES

And a piece of New York dies with it: Pages 2 & 3

Above: ***Kevorkian after his arrest and bail for assisting in the suicide of Thomas Hyde Jnr.***

condition warrants it, despite anything else. That's what a doctor should do. All these silly religious nuts. All these people, they don't care about suffering humanity. They hate what I am doing. They don't talk about suffering patients. If I were Satan and I was helping a suffering person end his life, would that make a difference? Any person who does this is going to have an image problem'.

THE DEPRESSION FACTOR

Some medical experts claim that Kevorkian is killing people because they are depressed, and not because of their disease. 'What he is doing is killing people because they are depressed', said James Boop, an Indiana attorney. 'But depression is curable. He takes absolutely no account of this. He's not qualified to diagnose depression nor is he qualified to treat it'.

Yet Kevorkian remains steadfast, claiming that in some cases, the severe depression his patients feel can sometimes justify suicide. 'You can't dope up a quadriplegic', he told an interviewer. 'There's no pain to alleviate, but the anguish in the head is immense, especially after five or ten years of lying on your back looking up at the ceiling'. Moreover, he claims many of his critics have no idea of what these people are going through, and would gladly meet them in debate. 'I will argue with them if they will allow themselves to be strapped into a wheelchair for 72 hours so they can't move, and they are catheterised and they are placed on the toilet and fed and bathed. Then they can sit in a chair and debate with me.'

SOME DOCTORS ADMIT THAT KEVORKIAN IS VIEWED BY MANY AMERICANS AS A REASONABLE ALTERNATIVE TO MODERN MEDICINE

Even some doctors who disagree with his methods reluctantly admit, however, that Kevorkian is viewed by many Americans as a reasonable alternative to modern medicine, which can be cold and uncaring. Professor George Annas, from the prestigious Boston University School of Medicine, told reporters: 'First we don't tell them they are dying. We do tell them their diagnosis and all the alternative treatments available. But we don't tell them their prognosis. We tell them, "You have cancer, and you can have surgery, radiation, chemotherapy, or all three together, or even any two". We don't tell them that no matter what we do, it's almost certain they are going to die soon'. Moreover, Annas says too many doctors simply ignore their patients' pain. 'Up to 90 per cent of patients die in too much pain. Some doctors actually argue that their patients are going to get addicted. But they can't have thought about it for more than two minutes to say something like that. The vast majority simply don't know how to treat pain, and they don't think that it is important. They want to cure the person. Death is still seen as the enemy. And that's what Kevorkian throws in their face. What he says is, "Some people want death, and I am going to give it to them".'

THE MORAL POSITION

Kevorkian is so adamant about his moral position, that even while the ACLU challenge to the Michigan ban against assisted-suicide wended it way through the courts, he was there for his 16th suicide. That came on 16 May 1993, when Ronald Mansur, a real estate man with bone and lung cancer, killed himself using carbon monoxide. Police found the body – after an 'anonymous' call – at the real estate office. 'He was in hell', a long time friend said. 'He would cry on the phone'.

Kevorkian was promptly arrested, but stung by earlier charges and arrests, refused to tell authorities what had happened. He would only allow that he had indeed been present and had watched as Mansur ended his life by inhaling carbon monoxide. However, he offered no details about his role in the death. After he was finger-printed, Kevorkian was released. While local officials contemplated charging him yet again, the Michigan law outlawing assisted suicide was overturned. They have no choice but to drop all charges.

'We think the statute violated people's privacy rights', commented an ACLU spokesman when the decision to overturn the ban was announced.

At the time of writing, Mansur was Kevorkian's last assisted suicide. But now that the law has been struck down, it is probably only a matter of time before his name again surfaces in connection with the suicide of another gravely ill person.

Whether he is indeed a ghoulish real-life incarnation of Dr Frankenstein or a medical crusader cannot be fully answered at this time. Only history can decide for sure how he will be remembered, or what effect his foray into hitherto forbidden territory will mean for future generations.

Below: ***Accused of murder in the deaths of two women, the strain appears to be beginning to tell on Kevorkian.***

THEODOR MORELL
Hitler's Doctor

The Third Reich's leading quack doctor Theodor Morell dispensed an extensive pharmacopeia of comical and sinister medicines to many leading members of the Nazi hierarchy. His main patient was Hitler himself.

In the pantheon of Nazi leaders there were many sycophants and flunkies, each one of them jostling for power at the elbow of their beloved Fuehrer, Adolf Hitler. There was Heinrich Himmler, the former chicken farmer who became the head of the most infamous elite guard of all time, the SS There was fat Hermann Goering, corpulent, flamboyant, but with a heart blacker than coal. There was Martin Bormann, the sinister party secretary who perhaps more than any general or Nazi party official knew the inner workings of Hitler's twisted mind.

But there was one other, less visible member of the Nazi coterie whose power derived not from some high office or exalted title, but from the well-being of the Fuehrer himself. His name was Dr Theodor Morell and he served his leader as personal physician right up until his suicide at the end of the war. Like many other doctors of the Third Reich, Theodor Morell sold out his Hippocratic Oath by keeping alive mankind's vilest tormentor. He pumped the Nazi dictator full with drugs of dubious merit and poisoned his reasoning with tales of semi-mystical quackery. In a way, Morell may well have deserved a medal for his services – from the Allies. For it's widely recognised that he was a hack of the highest order, an unskilled, semi-literate buffoon whose potions probably served to weaken Adolf Hitler rather than strengthen him. Theodor Morell stands alone in the chronicles of wicked doctors as a man who believed what he was doing was right, when everyone else in the gangster milieu which was Hitler's court saw him as the impostor he was. Only the fear of offending Der Fuehrer stopped them from ever speaking out against such witchcraft as performed by the good 'Herr Doktor'.

A post-war interrogation of a Nazi official produced this very unflattering portrait of the physician that others who were in Hitler's inner circle dubbed Dr Feel Good: 'He was portly, very obese, cringing in his manner to Hitler and others in the immediate circle of the leader.

'He was inarticulate in speech, gross in manner and known by all as a quack. Reichsmarshall Hermann Goering called him "Herr Reich Injection Master" because

Above: ***Heinrich Himmler, leader of the SS, who was intensely jealous of Dr Theodor Morell's closeness to Adolf Hitler.***

Opposite: ***Dr Theodor Morell, chief physician of Adolf Hitler.***

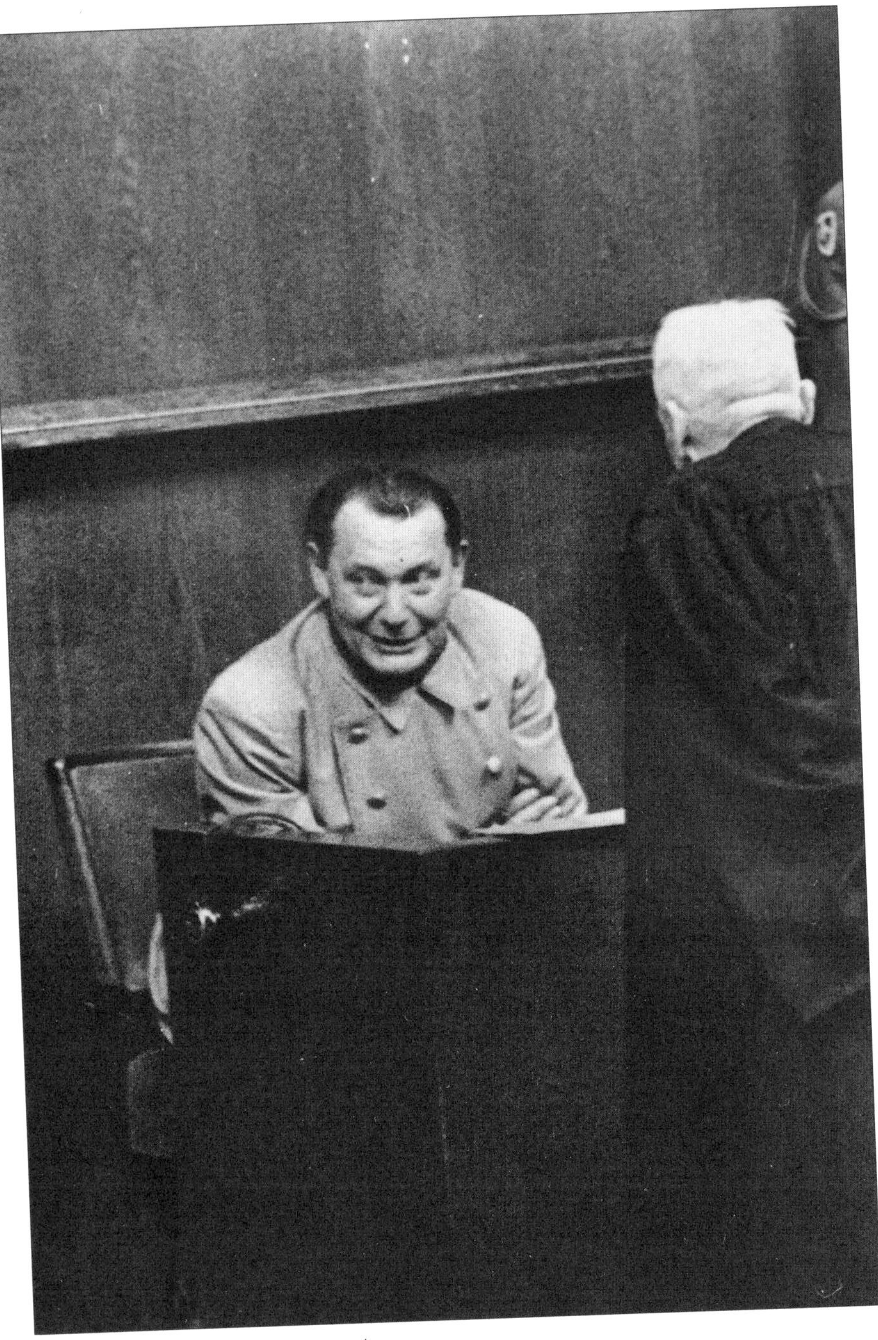

Above: ***Hermann Goering, humbled at Nuremberg. Like all top Nazis, he paid lip service to the powerful Morell.***

Opposite Top Left: ***Crown Prince Willy, son of Kaiser Wilhelm, was one of Herr Doktor's first patients.***

Opposite Far Right: ***The compulsive, obsessive, maniacally evil Adolf Hitler became entranced by Morell.***

it seemed to all who came into contact with him that he could cure the ills of the world with a few well placed hypodermic syringes'.

Little is known of Morell's early life in Berlin where he was born to merchant parents. But he was a diligent student who passed entrance examinations to the city's medical school where he applied himself for seven long years of study before qualifying as a physician. He then travelled to study at the Pasteur Institute in Paris where the great Russian bacteriologist Ilya Mechnikov mesmerised him in studies about bacterial infection, immunisation and the spread of communicable diseases.

It was in the early 1930s, just at the time that Nazism was beginning to grow like a bacillus in the body politic of German society, that Morell began his medical career. He started as a ship's doctor on cruise liners going to America, but soon decided that going into business for himself was the only sure way to make money – and money was far more important to Morell than any lofty notions about serving his fellow man. He practised medicine in Munich for a time before returning to Berlin where he opened a surgery on the Kurfurstendamm, the central thoroughfare of the old Imperial city that was comparable in status and charm to the Champs Elysees in Paris. Above the door to his practice he hung the sign: 'Dr. T. Morell, Practitioner in Medicine, specialising in Skin and Venereal Diseases'. A short time as an intern had taught him that sexually transmitted diseases were rife and that people – many of them rich and famous – were willing to pay handsome sums to be treated quietly, discreetly – and quickly.

MORELL'S WAY IN

One of his patients was the former German Crown Prince, known to a generation of British servicemen during the Great War as 'Little Willy.' Willy's patronage – he was actually treated for a nervous condition, not for any sexual infection – ensured Morell the entree to society that he craved so much. Soon they were beating a path to his door, the rich and famous, wealthy and influential. And among the patients were the vanguard of the new society that was rapidly taking over all aspects of life in Germany – the Nazis.

Morell, blessed with an innate ability to cast his lot in with those he perceived to be on the winning side, soon built up a clientele of Nazi party officials and functionaries. Word was circulating in the highest echelons of the party that, in Morell, there had come to Berlin a sorcerer capable of performing miracles upon the human body. In actuality, he offered treatment that was available in every public hospital – except, like the huckster he was, he dressed it up as some kind of miracle 'breakthrough.' He routinely bought up the collections of medicine bottles and jars of old pharmaceutical companies and placed them in his office to give himself the aura of an alchemist!

It was in 1935, with the sickness of a photographer called Heinrich Hoffmann, that Morell came to the attention of the nation's Fuehrer. Hoffmann, the court photographer, had caught a chill in the chilly mountain air of the Berghof, Hitler's Bavarian retreat, which had grown into pneumonia. Several highly placed Nazi officials insisted that Hoffman be treated by the miraculous Dr Morell, now ensconced as the toast of Berlin. With Hoffmann when he came for treatment was a young woman called Eva Braun – fresh faced, lively, beautiful even. He could not know then that she would die with her beloved Fuehrer in the ruins of Berlin in just ten years time.

THE ROUTE TO THE TOP

Again using standard medicines of the day, Morell was able to treat Hoffmann successfully. But in him – and in Eva Braun, the friend who accompanied him – Morell had found the person with direct access to the most powerful man on the European continent. Soon would follow the top functionaries of the party – and in their wake, Adolf Hitler himself.

Albert Speer, the party architect and a man recognised as probably the most sane of the clique which surrounded Hitler, fell

under Morell's spell first. He had his reservations, but felt that he ought to go for fear of offending the Fuehrer's top officials. Suffering from intestinal disorders, largely brought on by overwork in designing the new capital 'Germania' which Hitler wanted to call Berlin, he sought Morell out early in 1936. Later he would' write; 'My stomach and circulation rebelled against an irrational working rhythm and adjustment to Hitler's abnormal habits. I called at Morell's private office and after a superficial examination he prescribed for me his intestinal bacteria drugs, dextrose, vitamins and hormone tablets.

Above: ***Heinrich Hoffmann, Hitler's court photographer, with his wife and stepdaughter at Nuremberg.***

Opposite Top: ***At the court of the Fuehrer, Morell (arrowed) stands behind the Nazi elite.***

Opposite Bottom: ***The portly Morell shakes the hand of his Messiah as he receives the hero's award of the Knight's Cross.***

A SECOND OPINION

'For safety's sake I afterwards had a thorough examination by Professor von Bergmann, the specialist in internal medicine at Berlin University. I was found not to be suffering from any organic trouble, as Morell had stated, but only from nervous symptoms caused by overwork. I then slowed my pace down as best I could. The symptoms abated. To avoid offending Hitler and the others I carefully pretended that I was following Morell's instructions to the letter. And since my health improved, I became for a time Morell's showpiece'. Speer did not dare write these words until the 1960s when he was freed from a 20-year jail term imposed at Nuremberg. He, an intellectual, remained silent for fear of offending the star-struck Fuehrer.

HITLER WAS A CHRONIC HYPOCHONDRIAC THROUGHOUT HIS LIFE, SEEKING DEMONS WHERE NONE EXISTED

THE LONG-SUFFERING LEADER

Hitler is believed to have first visited him in the same year as Speer, although such records were lost in the bombing which reduced Berlin to little more than brickdust. Hitler suffered massively from intestinal trouble throughout his life, probably brought on by the mustard and phosgene gassings he suffered as a soldier at the front in the Great War. A company runner charged with getting messages to and from the front line while under fire, he finished the war as a temporarily blinded casualty of the conflict. On top of his stomach ailments, at the time he saw Morell, he was suffering from a foot rash – probably nothing more than athlete's foot – but Morell saw the opportunity to bamboozle the impressionable Fuehrer with nonsensical twaddle. He said the stomach problems and his foot rash were linked, that one was a symptom of the other because Der Fuehrer had lost vital 'intestinal flora' as a result of inhaling gas during the war. As Hitler lay on his examination table, the Gestapo guards situated just feet away, Morell pumped him with a drug he invented called 'Multflor' which consisted of intestinal bacteria gathered from Bulgarian bulls! Then he gave him several more injections of vitamins, hormones, phosphorus, dextrose and a cortisone-type drug.

A CURE FOR HITLER

Within days Hitler found himself cured of both ailments – but it's highly unlikely that Morell's potions had anything to do with his recovery. Hitler was a chronic hypochondriac throughout his life. Psychologists in the post war years have analysed his condition ad infinitum, coming to the conclusion that he sought demons where none existed and then celebrated like a demented child when they were banished. With his foot rash gone and his stomach pains vanquished, he proclaimed: 'Nobody has ever told me before, in such clear and precise terms, exactly what was wrong with me. His method of cure is so logical that I have the greatest confidence in him. I shall follow his prescriptions to the letter and shall urge all those who are dearest to me to place their health and well-being into his gifted hands.'

Hitler suddenly took on the living habits of a Franciscan monk. Used to eating sausage and drinking beer, and sometimes a little of the Bavarian wine called Frankenwein, he now became a teetotaller and vegetarian. He hired a vegetarian cook, Frau Manzialy, who was to stay with him until the end, even preparing his last meal before suicide in the bunker in 1945. He banished the heavy chocolate cakes and Linzertorte that had graced his tables since his earliest days and cut out the whipped cream which used to drown out his rich coffee. 'How lucky!' he proclaimed to Himmler at a private audience, 'How lucky that I was able to meet Morell. He has saved my life'. The good doctor was well on his way to beatification from the highest priest of Nazism.

Above: ***The portly Morell on the cover of a pro-Nazi medical journal.***

HIS WIFE WATCHED HIM CHANGE INTO A BROODING, SILENT MONSTER. HE WOULD LOOK AT HER WITH THOSE EYES...

Patronage from Hitler opened many more doors and brought the doctor great riches from various Reich ministries, which he was careful to salt away in bank accounts in Zurich and Geneva. He patented a flea powder for use by the Wehrmacht which was ordered by the ton. Examination of it after the war proved it to be 90 percent chalk with a smattering of household insecticide. He marketed pills which promised an increase in potency and they were bought by the bucketful by the S.S., which was in the market for fertile young men to breed blond, blue-eyed babies with Aryan maidens for the 1000 year Reich. There is no evidence to suggest they were any more effective than ground rhinoceros horn. And there were the high and mighty of Nazism, each one keen to be treated – and to be seen to be treated – by the Fuehrer's favourite.

On 3 September 1939, the day that Britain declared war on Germany over her invasion two days earlier of Poland, a young, infatuated British maiden called Unity Mitford shot herself on a park bench in the middle of Munich's English Garden. Infatuated by Hitler since his early days, she suddenly seemed to have had a massive conversion back to reality when she saw that the end result of the flags and the banners and the massed 'Sieg Heils' translated into conquest and war and death. Hitler was beside himself with anguish – he had great affection for the upper-class English beauty whom he nurtured because of her fawning admiration. He summoned Morell to treat her in a luxury government clinic, to give her the best care possible. Soon Unity Mitford, lying in a coma, resembled a pin cushion due to the myriad drugs and serums he pumped into her. In eight months of continuous care her condition did not change one iota. Finally, in May 1940, Hitler sent her back to England via Switzerland. Doctors who received her back in Britain were appalled by the treatment she had received – they thought that the injections had actually accelerated her ill health rather than helping to cure it. She died in 1948 – a victim of Morell's hocus-pocus as much as the bullet that she tried to end her life with.

FEARS OF A POPULATION

It remains a conundrum whether Morell really believed the potions he peddled were effective in fighting illness, or whether he was a true cynic who knew he was merely cashing in on the foibles and fears of a population looking for life's elixir. With hindsight, it is almost certain that it was the latter. As the heady years of victory in the war turned into the bitter years of defeat, Morell was called upon increasingly to administer to Hitler an ever-more baffling cocktail of drugs. Included among them was a serum derived from bulls testicles, mixed with the hormones from young salamander lizards! Others included: Brom-Nervacit, consisting of potassium bromide, sodium barbitone and aminopyrinen, all mixed together and injected into the abdomen to promote rest; camomile enemas, sympatol which included ethanol tartrate to promote an increased heartbeat and Glyconorm, a mixture of enzymes to ease digestion and reduce Hitler's chronic flatulence.

There was septoid, for respiratory infections and hardened arteries, vitamins in a cocktail he called Intelan to stimulate his declining appetite, Eukadol, to stop his spasms and Omnadin, an animal-fat based serum devised to ward off colds. Any doctor examining this shopping list of quackery now would shake his head in astonishment and incredulity.

As the war raged on Hitler's moods and his general health condition deteriorated with each passing defeat. His monstrous rages were – several of his entourage believed – brought on because of the massive amounts of drugs Morell continued to pump into his weakened frame. General Heinz Guderian, his most brilliant Blitzkrieg tactician, saw the Fuehrer after he had received a dozen Morell injections before breakfast. His animal rage knew no bounds when Guderian tried to point out to him the hopelessness on a certain battle front. The general recalled: 'He raised his fist, his cheeks were flushed with rage and his whole body was trembling. He stood in front of me, beside himself with fury and having literally lost all control. After each outburst he would suddenly stride up and down the carpet then suddenly stop before me and hurl his next accusation in my face. He was almost screaming, his eyes popping out of his head, the veins standing out on his temples'.

After July 1944 and the attempt on his life at his Wolf's Lair command centre in Rastenburg, east Prussia, Hitler went on his final downhill. The bomb planted beneath a map table by a German officer involved in the plot to rid Germany of her greatest bane killed several high-ranking officers but spared the life of the Fuehrer. Within hours Morell was flown to Rastenburg where he administered no fewer than 15 injections within 40 minutes of arrival!

POISONOUS PILLS

A physician called Karl Brandt, who had attended to Hitler when Morell was not available, seems to have been one of the few – perhaps the only individual – who had the courage to speak with him about the effects of the 'medicine' being prescribed by Morell. He tested some ear pills that he was giving Hitler for damage sustained in the Rastenburg explosion – and found them to contain harmful levels of poison. Brandt

AS THE WAR RAGED ON, HITLER'S MOODS AND HIS GENERAL HEALTH CONDITION DETERIORATED WITH EACH DEFEAT

MORELL ADMINISTERED NO FEWER THAN 15 INJECTIONS TO HITLER WITHIN 40 MINUTES OF ARRIVING TO TREAT HIM

Below: ***One table away from his master, Morell is close by as Hitler entertains the top echelon of the Nazi party.***

attempted to broach the subject with Hitler, backed up with the findings of an independent university researcher who concurred that Morell's potions were indeed harming his life. Hitler would have none of it. He told him: 'You can say what you will about Morell. He is and always will be my personal physician. I have full confidence in him – he is the only man of medicine who has ever fully understood me'. What Morell understood quite clearly was the hypochondria that afflicted Hitler, a condition that turned to massive paranoia and psychosis as the war ground on.

A DIRTY QUACK

Another person close to Hitler, Eva Braun, had initially believed in the quackery but later became repelled by him. She was disgusted by Morell's personal habits, his 'pig-sty' office and dirty fingernails. During quiet moments she too tried to wean the man she loved from dependency on Morell's elixirs. She too failed.

IN THE BERLIN BUNKER MORELL CARRIED OUT HIS LAST DEMENTED PRACTICES ON HITLER'S WRETCHED FRAME

Below: ***The doomed Unity Mitford (second right) at an Anglo-German Fellowship Meeting in 1938. With her are her parents (left) and Dr Fitz-Randolph, a German embassy official.***

Late in 1944 Morell drew up an entire diet for the Fuehrer based on mushrooms. He convinced Hitler that mushrooms were rich in the vitamins he needed and even persuaded Hitler to part with millions of Reichsmarks for a greenhouse at Berchtesgarten to grow them in. But Hitler was never to return to his summer eyrie as defeat loomed ever nearer and the glasshouse remained as another folly to yet another madcap scheme in which he indulged the crazy doctor.

It was in the phantasmagorical, troglodyte world of the Berlin bunker, the subterranean bolthole for Hitler and the last remaining acolytes of his crumbling empire, that Morell carried out his last demented practices upon the wretched frame of the now desperately-ill Fuehrer. His left side shook uncontrollably, his right leg, damaged in the Rastenburg blast, dragged uselessly behind him. He frothed at the mouth in terrifying rages that could last up to 30 minutes – and then slumped, drained, in his chair, staring blankly ahead,

oblivious to all around. All, that is, except Morell. In his remaining time left on this earth Hitler requested and received ever larger dosages of the drugs prescribed by his physician. Karl Brandt was in the bunker too, despite his earlier attempts to put Hitler off Morell's kind of care-giving. He treated Hitler in the final weeks while Morell slept, or if he needed something straightforward, like an aspirin or tranquilisers for sleep.

THE END DRAWS NEAR

Brandt was appalled at the human guinea-pig that he believed Morell had turned the national leader into. He confronted him in the surgery of the bunker one afternoon, six weeks before Hitler ended his life. He told him: 'His face is pallid, his eyes are weak, clouded, he cannot stop shaking and he can hardly stand during conference. I put it to you that you are doing the Fuehrer more harm than good'.

But Morell, who was also doling out massive quantities of his moonshine medicine to assorted party officials, soldiers and SS bigwigs sheltering in the bunker before the final 'Gotterdammerung', laughed in his face. He was incredibly wealthy, thanks to his secret bank accounts, he enjoyed the patronage of Hitler and he was not guilty of any war crimes. He knew that he, at least, would walk out alive from the mousetrap of Berlin, no matter who arrived to conquer the city first.

But to pay back the insolent doctor he was instrumental in whispering poison into Hitler's ear. Brandt, he told him, had sent his wife and child into an area of Germany that was about to be overrun by allied forces. This was tantamount to treason for the deranged Hitler and he ordered Brandt's summary court martial followed by execution. Brandt was spared only by the direct intervention of S.S. chief Himmler, but the episode proved who remained closest to Hitler right up until the final moments.

Above: ***Dr Karl Brandt, another of Hitler's physicians, appearing before an allied tribunal.***

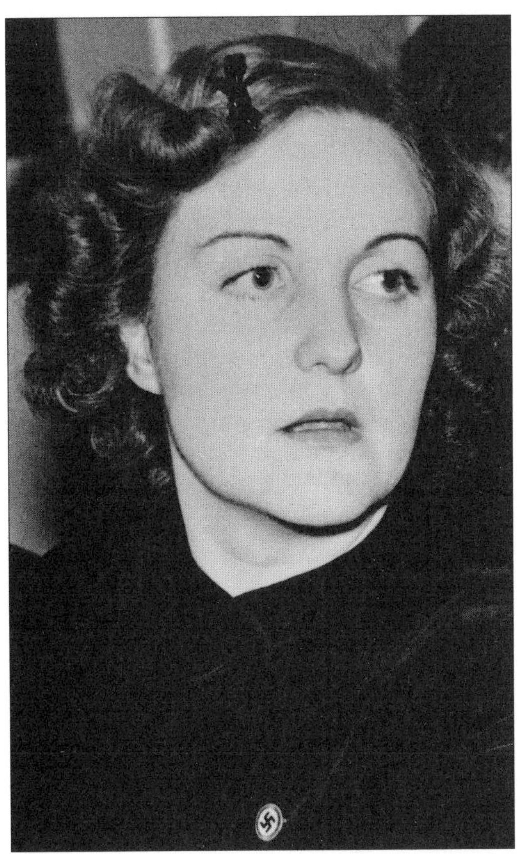

Left: ***Unity Mitford, the English aristocrat who fell under the Nazis' spell. Hitler placed her under the care of Morell.***

HITLER REQUESTED AND RECEIVED EVER LARGER DOSAGES OF THE DRUGS PRESCRIBED BY HIS PHYSICIAN

Above: ***The bed in the Fuhrer's shelter, where Hitler and Eva Braun are alleged to have poisoned themselves.***

Opposite Top: ***Morell, grinning behind the Fuehrer, in Poland in 1939.***

Opposite Bottom: ***Morell receives a War Work cross for devotion to science from an unsmiling SS aide.***

THE MILLIONS MORELL MADE FROM FLEA POWDER AND FROM TREATING GENERALS AND MOVIE STARS WERE NEVER SPENT

One of his most diabolical acts of the whole war came two days before the Fuehrer and Eva Braun were to commit suicide. Magda Goebbels, unable to live with her beloved Fuehrer gone, asked him for poison to end her life and those of her six children. Morell, who had long ago forgotten the ethics of his Hippocratic Oath, supplied her with the poison. All died in the charnel house, including Goebbels himself, and all were cremated outside the bunker, in shell holes caused by the Russian artillery that ground the once beautiful capital city into ruins.

On 20 April, Hitler's birthday, the leader surfaced one more time above ground to decorate some fanatical Hitler Youths with Iron Crosses. The youngsters, who had grown up only on cinematic and poster images of the Fuehrer, were shocked at his ghostly appearance. Stooped, shaking uncontrollably, he patted them on the cheeks as if they were his own sons, before scurrying back underground with a man clutching a doctor's bag following close behind him. Dr Theodor Morell was about to give his last consultation for the individual who had caused the deaths of some 50 million people in the global war.

After injecting Hitler with vitamin K and bacterial enzymes for one last time, he was told to flee the city along with an assortment of secretaries and minor officials. Morell, his eyes gleaming with the thought of untouched loot awaiting him in Switzerland, did not need to be told twice to go. While he was certainly cringing to Hitler, scheming in his methods to stay close by him, he was never a Nazi zealot. Dr Morell only ever worked towards one end in his treatment of Hitler and the other Nazi fatcats – the betterment of Dr Morell. Clutching his assorted potions he fled the bunker and headed west, away from the advancing Russians.

But fate played a just trick on the evil old quack. Just when he thought he was safe, having been captured by Americans and placed in an internment camp, he died in May 1948 from TB and heart failure. The millions he earned from flea powder, from treating generals, movie stars, the

Crown Prince and Hitler himself, were never spent.

Dr Peter Masterson, an American historian who has made a study of Morell, said: 'It was a fitting end to a man who betrayed the very ethics of medicine. While he might not have carried out medical experiments like some Nazi doctors, he was, nevertheless, a rogue and a scoundrel who, some believe, deserved to hang for supplying the poison which snuffed out the lives of the Goebbels children.

WEAKENING HITLER

'But in a curious way perhaps it is the allies who should thank Dr. Morell for turning Adolf Hitler into a wretched shell of a creature, someone who was drastically unable to prosecute the conduct of the war due to his weakened state.

'History's judgement is that Morell was nothing more than a confidence man who used a stethoscope and pills to con his patients into believing he was something more than mortal'.

KARL BABOR
Royal Doctor of Death

In World War II, Karl Babor had been an SS doctor at Treblinka and Auschwitz concentration camps, but after the fall of Germany he slipped through Allied hands and made a new life in Ethiopia, where he became a physician at the imperial court. For years he lived well, but his past was determined to catch up with him.

In Addis Ababa, the old colonial-style capital of Ethiopia, they called him Herr Doktor. Herr Doktor had come from the old world to this new frontier where his courtly charm and urbane ways had marked him out as a man of culture and distinction. His manners were not lost on the Emperor Haile Selassie or members of his family who took him under their wing. Soon he was doctor by appointment to the court of

Above: ***His Imperial Majesty Haile Selassie, emperor of Ethiopia, who gave sanctuary to Dr Babor.***

Left: ***Addis Ababa, which Babor came to call home, was vastly different to the Europe he left behind.***

Opposite: ***Karl Babor, camp doctor of the Gross Rosen concentration camp, fled to Africa.***

HERR DOKTOR SPOKE TO THOSE HE MET ON THE COCKTAIL CIRCUIT OF HIS DESIRE TO AID HIS FELLOW MAN

Left: ***Josef Mengele, the camp doctor of Auschwitz, who was supreme arbiter of life and death over millions.***

Below: ***The camp gates at Auschwitz bearing the hollow legend, 'Work Brings Freedom'.***

the Emperor. Herr Doktor, German by birth, had come to the east African country in the aftermath of the Second World War. To those he met on the cocktail circuit or in the missions he spoke of his desire to aid his fellow man. Oh yes, he could have stayed in Germany and made a great deal of money in private practice, he frequently said. But his calling was here, where he was most needed. Not only did he look after the health of the Emperor and his brood, he also donated his free time to the Menelik Hospital, a state-of-the-art institution equipped with first-class machinery and medicines given to the nation by the Soviet Union. He was a dark blond man with sad eyes, eyes which were rumoured to have gazed upon much sorrow. Indeed they had – and the sorrow was caused by the brain and hands and heart of their owner. The good doctor was none other

than Karl Babor and his trade in the war was mass murder.

Dr Karl Babor was one of that select band of Nazi war criminals for whom there must undoubtedly be reserved a special place in hell. Like Josef Mengele, the demented medic of Auschwitz who performed bizarre experiments on twins as he sought to produce a master race of blue-eyed, blond supermen for his Fuehrer, Babor conveniently ditched his Hippocratic Oath for the pursuit of pain and suffering. A fervent member of the Nazi Party since the early days of Hitler, he later joined the SS where he knew that his medical training could be put to good use. He was not even a fully qualified doctor when he joined the black order; he had served six of seven years at the Vienna University medical centre. But six out of seven was good enough for the Nazis. They were always seeking intellectuals, scholars and doctors to their ranks to give credibility to what was an otherwise absurd band of misfits and deadbeats. Babor fitted the mould well.

Above: ***Vienna, the Austrian capital, home of the woman who would play a vital part in tracing him.***

MENGELE PERFORMED BIZARRE EXPERIMENTS ON TWINS AS HE SOUGHT TO PRODUCE A MASTER RACE FOR THE FUEHRER

DEADLY VISITS

When the concentration camp network was assembled throughout Germany – and later in the conquered lands – Babor found himself assigned to many centres as medical officer and later camp doctor. On the side of the living he innoculated a few SS men, stitched a few wounds, punctured a few abscesses. On the side of the dead he moved like a grim blond reaper. A visit from the good doctor to places like Dachau and Buchenwald meant death – usually by an injection through the heart. He killed to collect human tissue for bizarre experiments that had no scientific value. He killed because he wanted to examine brains for mental disorders. Chiefly, though, he killed because he enjoyed it. His most notorious reign was at Treblinka, man for man, child for child, the worst death camp of them all. Treblinka, near Warsaw, was in full service for the Reich for a little over a year and in that time some 700,000 people were executed. There were only 40 survivors at the war's end. Just how many Dr Babor snuffed out with his syringe and his scalpel will never be fully known.

THE HUMAN ABATTOIR

But after Treblinka was closed down in 1943, with the more efficient, and still more deadly, Auschwitz camp going on stream as the premier human abattoir, Babor found himself at the Grossrosen concentration camp near Breslau – later Wroclaw – in Poland. Here there would be a man who could bear witness to what he had done – someone who was to become the conscience, the soul and the avenger for all the victims of Nazism, wherever and however they had died. Simon Wiesenthal was in Grossrosen in 1944, the time of the Third Reich's greatest defeats on the battlefield. But they still had time for their war against the innocent and unarmed, those who could not fight back. Wiesenthal, who

Above: ***Scenes from the Warsaw Ghetto uprising. Hitler fuelled the crematoria of his death camps with victims like these.***

'THE FAINT SMELL OF BURNED FLESH IS IN THE AIR. THE YEAR IS 1944. THE TIME MIGHT BE ANY TIME OF DAY OR NIGHT'

THE CREMATORIUM IS SERVED BY A RUSSIAN PRISONER CALLED BLACK IVAN. FEW PRISONERS SEE HIM WHILE THEY ARE ALIVE

has devoted his life to bringing to justice the perpetrators of the Holocaust, said in his memoirs: 'There is a certain scene on the stage of my memory I shall never forget. It is a small room with dark grey walls. The entrance is on the left side. The exit is in the middle of the back wall. The exit leads straight into the crematorium of the Grossrosen concentration camp.

HORRIFIC MEMORIES

'On the otherwise empty stage is a small table with several syringes and a few bottles filled with a colourless liquid. There is one chair. The faint smell of burned flesh is in the air. The year is 1944. The time might be any time of day or night. This is the antechamber of the Grossrosen crematorium. There are no gas chambers in this concentration camp. The crematorium is served by a Russian prisoner called Black Ivan, because constant smoke has blackened his face and his hands. Ivan looks really terrible, but few inmates ever see him while they are still alive. By the time Black Ivan gets to them they no longer know any fear.

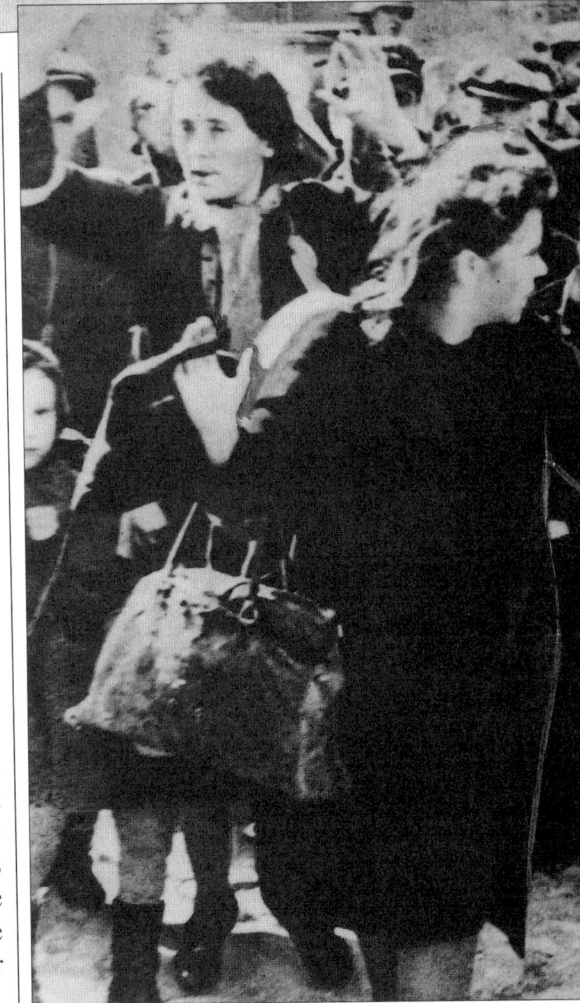

He carries their ashes to a nearby field where the camp gardeners plant vegetables for the camp kitchen, for fertilizer. I know all this because I was a prisoner assigned to work in the vegetable garden.

'Now a young man stands in the middle of the room. He wears a white doctor's coat on top of his SS uniform. Most prisoners have seen the young "doctor" before; he is a member of the "selection committee". When the transports arrive, the prisoners are ordered to walk down the ramp and stand at attention at a small table. The "doctor" at the table moves his index finger to the right – life – or to the left, death. An SS man makes a sign on a list. The "doctor" takes a second look at the human wreck before him. "Open your mouth! Wider!" He nods. The prisoner is not entirely worthless. Three gold fillings. The "doctor" marks a big black cross with a thick wet pencil on the prisoner's forehead. "*Abtreten!*" All marked people must register at the camp office. The gold fillings in

Above and Left: ***A Russian Orthodox priest and a little boy from the Warsaw Ghetto. Both were enemies in the eyes of the SS and had to be exterminated like vermin.***

THE 'DOCTOR' MOVES HIS INDEX FINGER TO THE RIGHT – LIFE – OR TO THE LEFT, DEATH. AN SS MAN MAKES A SIGN ON A LIST

their mouths are registered in duplicate. They no longer own them but are permitted to use them while they're alive.

'Soon the prisoners directed to the left will stand again in front of the young man in the white medical coat. He is highly skilled at his job. He fills the syringe, tells the patient (who is stripped to his navel) to sit down on the chair. The patient is held by two SS men. The young man quickly steps in front of him, injects the lethal needle into his heart with a sharp thrust. The syringe contains phenolic acid.

DEADLY DOSES

'"Herr Doktor Babor" is well liked by his SS superiors, who call him Herr Doktor. "I always like to give them a little more than the lethal dose, just to be sure", he has told them. The "Doktor" is a very humane man. Sometimes prisoners are frightened when he administers the phenolic coup de grace, but they haven't got much time to think. Other patients are waiting. The bodies of the dead are speedily dragged out through the exit door. A little later people will see smoke come out of the chimney. How often had I seen the smoke come out of the chimney while I was working in the camp garden? It was only the will of God that I had not had to sit down on the chair in front of "Herr Doktor" Karl Babor'.

Babor was caught by the allies at the end of the war. But in the maelstrom of Europe, as the big fish were hunted down, many like him escaped. He spent several months in 1947 at the Landesgericht Prison in Vienna, but the evidence against him was judged 'insuffficent' by allied war crimes hunters who were swamped with the monstrous details of what had occurred in occupied Europe during the war. The following year he resumed his studies at Vienna. After having despatched God knows how many souls to meet their maker during the war, he finally made it to being a doctor, swearing 'to serve all humanity' when he accepted his qualifications in the Great Hall of the University.

After an internship at a local hospital he moved to the Alpine town of Gmunden where he settled into the cosy life of a provincial doctor. But his past was already catching up with him. In 1952 allied hunters called on his parents' apartment in Vienna. They had had a special brief to track down personnel who worked at Treblinka. The awful details of the camp were now becoming clearer. His parents tipped him off and he vanished, fleeing to Africa with his wife Bobo and daughter Dagmar. There, in Ethiopia, where westerners and their medicine were always welcome, he inveigled his way into the royal family and became the doctor for other notables. But the memory of the war years and what he had done would never leave him. Slowly, surely, his conscience began to eat away at him like an incurable cancer.

ANIMAL BEHAVIOUR

At night came the nightmares. His daughter Dagmar would later recount how he howled at the moon before sloping off to the jungle to join the animals that he counted more as friends and comrades than any homo sapiens. Chief friend among these 'friends' were the crocodiles; perhaps because, like him, they were cold, calculating killers who had evolved perfectly since the age of the dinosaurs to survive. Unlike him, they had no conscience.

Opposite Top and Bottom: ***The now overgrown ground of the Auschwitz extermination camp where three million people perished.***

HE HOWLED AT THE MOON BEFORE SLOPING OFF TO THE JUNGLE TO JOIN THE ANIMALS THAT HE COUNTED AS HIS FRIENDS

Below: ***Human cargoes gave men like Babor ample supplies for his grotesque, twisted experiments.***

Wiesenthal, and other Nazi hunters, were desperate to find him but had no idea of his whereabouts. He was spirited out of Germany with the aid of the ODESSA – the organisation of former members of the SS – which set him up with false papers and necessary travel documents. But once in Ethiopia Dr Babor learned three things which made him decide that an alias was no longer necessary by the mid-1950s. One was the fact that Ethiopia was so beautifully remote, far and away safer than other Nazi boltholes like South Africa and Argentina. Two, he enjoyed the patronage of the royal family and was therefore never likely to be sent back to hang at the end of a rope. And three, after ten years Ethiopian law stated that no foreigner could be sent back to face criminal charges in his own land or any other. Dr Babor breathed easy, safe in the knowledge that he would never be called to account for the many thousands he murdered.

But Wiesenthal had a stroke of luck in 1963 when a woman he refers to only as Ruth came to see him in his Vienna office. She had a remarkable tale to tell – one that would eventually lead to Dr Babor's suicide. It was a fantastic story that Wiesenthal prepared himself to listen to, but then he had heard many fantastic stories before in his never-ending role as the conscience and the avenger for the murdered. Ruth, who was Jewish, had decided to answer an advertisement one day placed by an Austrian overseas who wished to correspond with a woman with a view to marriage. The advertisement was placed by Dr Babor.

BABOR BELIEVED HE COULD NEVER BE BROUGHT TO ACCOUNT FOR THE MANY THOUSANDS HE HAD MURDERED

LONG-DISTANCE LOVE

The first reply was not from Babor but from an engineer in Vienna who had placed the advertisement on Babor's behalf. It was, in fact, his father, and he wrote seeking a meeting with Ruth so he could better explain the kind of women that his son was looking for and the kind of life she could expect in Ethiopia should she choose to correspond with him and finally travel to meet him. She agreed to write to Dr Karl Babor at Box 1761, Addis Ababa, and see where things might lead from there. The irony of her, a Jewess, writing to this sadist

Below: ***Confronting the immediate past, civilians are brought in to see the evil work wrought by the Nazis at the just-liberated Auschwitz death camp.***

who had killed so many of her fellow Jews, was, for the moment, lost on her. All she knew was that he was a brilliant doctor to the royal household who had lost his wife and was now feeling lonely. Soon the letters exchanged between them were becoming more intense, more romantic. Dr Babor wrote in a courtly, old-fashioned way that appealed to the soft nature of Ruth. He even sent a picture of himself to her. The eyes, the manic eyes which were the last thing that so many of his wretched victims saw on this earth, appeared 'like whirlpools' to her. She was falling in love with him.

FLYING SOUTH

Soon Dr Babor proposed a trip to Ethiopia and even sent her over a ticket. 'Please come', he wrote. 'My dear Ruth: I so want to see you here and to kiss your hand like I have kissed it a thousand times in my letters. I am sure you will like it here'. She agreed to go and Dagmar, his daughter studying in Paris, flew to Vienna to travel with her as she had not seen her father in two years.

Above: ***Israeli prime minister Rabin greets Beate Klarsefeld, the Nazi hunter, who exposed the freedom enjoyed in postwar Paris by a former top Gestapo official.***

BABOR OFFERED HIS PENPAL NEITHER FOOD NOR DRINK. INSTEAD, HE TOOK HER TO THE JUNGLE TO SEE HIS 'FRIENDS'

Once in Ethiopia any illusions that Ruth may have had about settling down to live happily ever after with the man of her dreams were cruelly shattered. At the airport where Dr Babor met her and Dagmar she judged him cold, calculating, almost sinister. He greeted her with barely a flicker' of warmth. 'It was as if he was thinking of something all the time, something from a very long time ago', said Ruth. 'Something deeply troubled this man to his very soul'.

Upon arriving at his modest home Dr Babor did not offer his penpal either food or drink; instead he took her into the jungle, off to see his 'friends'. They were the crocodiles lying in the fetid, brown water of a river, their red eyes glinting in the setting rays of the sun. On the way back Dr Babor pulled up outside a local police station and stuck his fist into the jaws of a domesticated old lion outside. It bit him, and Ruth noticed with discomfort how he seemed to enjoy watching the blood trickle down his arm. Later he drove back to his home and offered Ruth nothing but a cold can of corned beef for supper while he went to bed. She realised that she was in a for a very strange, a very sinister time.

Above: ***The emperor Haile Selassie with his wife. Thanks to Selassie's patronage, Babor became something of a celebrated resident of Ethiopia.***

'I HATE ALL HUMAN BEINGS. PEOPLE OUGHT TO BE GASSED – KILLED AS QUICKLY AS POSSIBLE', SHOUTED BABOR

The next story she recounted to Wiesenthal was an episode which seemed to fly in the face of all his alleged humanitarian instincts and codes as a doctor. The second night she was there a woman knocked on the door of his home clutching a sick child. His daughter Dagmar came for him and told him that he was needed. Babor jumped up and Ruth recalled: 'His eyes were bloodshot and his face was almost distorted with hatred. It was horrible. He shouted at Dagmar that he wouldn't touch the child, that he hated children; let them die. "I've never treated a child and I never will. Out with them!" Dagmar stood transfixed, silently pleading with me, and I said:"Karl, you're a doctor aren't you? That child is sick. Please go and take care of the baby". The good doctor Babor rounded on Ruth, told her she was a dirty fat Jewess, and for good measure added: 'I hate all human beings. People ought to be gassed – killed as quickly as possible. We don't need people. Animals are much better than people – animals must be spared'. He then fled to the Addis Ababa zoo where he spent the night stroking the dangerous wild cats as they slept.

Beate Klarsfeld, the Paris-based Nazi hunter, had already received a tip-off that Babor was in Africa and had, Wiesenthal suspected, found out that the bureaucracy there was interested in protecting a favoured son with connections to the Emperor. When she made enquiries about extraditing the good doctor to the west she was met with red tape, denials and finally official arrogance that, because he had committed no crimes there, he would never be eligible for extradition. After Ruth told her story to Wiesenthal – she fled from the house soon after the incident over the baby – he decided that the best way to get his hands on this most notorious of Nazi murderers might be to shame the government of Ethiopia. Ruth had come to Wiesenthal only on the suspicion of who he might be – she knew nothing of names like Treblinka or Grossrosen. It was Wiesenthal who fitted together the pieces of the jigsaw.

THE PRESS INVESTIGATE

To flush him out Wiesenthal staged a press conference with the Vienna correspondent of the *New York Times* – next to the London *Times*, probably the world's most influential newspaper. He told him the works – who Babor was, who he had been and what his crimes were. The repercussions were instant. From out of the Nazi abyss came forward victims, witnesses, survivors, collaborators – all who deluged the man who saw first-hand the smoke rising from the 'surgery' of this most infamous of Nazi killers. The Ethiopian government scrambled to deny that Babor was a doctor to the court – a denial later proven to be an outright lie. The revisionists argued that Babor had never been in Grossrosen, that Wiesenthal was picking on one minor cog in the whole grotesque machinery of Nazism, purely for personal reasons. And then there was the denial from Dr Babor himself. He set himself up at a press conference in Addis Ababa where he lied: 'I have never been in a concentration camp. I never experimented on prisoners. I was merely a military doctor during the war – a "truppenarzt"'. This was a mistake on his part as the full details of his SS membership, concentration camp service and medical history were available at the time through the Federal Prosecutor's office in Bonn.

FALSE DENIALS

Wiesenthal listened to Babor's denials with patience – the patience which has borne fruit in the pursuit and capture of hundreds of wartime murderers. Then he called his bluff – sending him an airline ticket to Austria together with a promise to pay his libel expenses if he instigated proceedings against him. Wiesenthal, in his book, *The Murderers Among Us*, wrote: 'In my cable I didn't think it tactful to add that room and board would be provided free of charge in the Landesgericht County Jail by the Austrian authorities who still had a warrant out for him. I gave the cable to the local newspapers in Addis Ababa – I didn't want him to be able to claim that he hadn't received it'.

But he received it all right. He just knew in his heart that he could never return to Austria.

Wiesenthal described the 'stage' of his memory upon which the cruel Dr Babor had appeared. It was now left for him to exit the drama of his appalling life for good. He drove into the jungle where he had taken Ruth upon her first night in Addis Ababa – the night when she was still contemplating marriage to this monster with the blood of innocents soaked upon his clothing. At the crocodile-infested river the beasts which earned his undying affection were milling about in the tepid waters, their red eyes glinting above the surface, their movements frightening the few water birds floating on the ripples. They ignored him as he waded out into the depths. When the water almost reached to his shoulders he levelled the hunting rifle he was carrying towards his heart, pulled the trigger, and slipped beneath the waves. Five days later a party of tourists discovered his body – even the crocs, it seemed, were choosy about what they ate.

Thousands of miles and another world away the flame of remembrance burned at the site of the Treblinka death camp, this most efficient engine of the Nazi extermination programme. The camp buildings are gone, the crematorium destroyed, the gas chambers long vanished. In the ground are the red brick foundations of the original camp and leading to it are the railroad tracks along which 700,000 people were brought to be liquidated – many of them by the needle and scalpel of Dr Karl Babor.

Ruth thought it ironic that she had nearly married him. She had relatives who had died in Treblinka. At least now, with the beast dead, she could say the Jewish holy prayer of Kaddish for their souls.

700,000 PEOPLE WERE LIQUIDATED, MANY OF THEM BY THE NEEDLE AND SCALPEL OF DR KARL BABOR

Below: ***It was in a river like this that Babor met his doom at the jaws of crocodiles.***

KLAUS FUCHS
The Traitorous Don

Left and Below: *Robert Oppenheimer, architect of America's atom bomb and the result of his brainchild, the aftermath of the Hiroshima bombing. The mushroom cloud rises above the doomed city in which 100,000 people died.*

Opposite: *Klaus Fuchs, the man who gave the secret of the atom bomb to the Russians.*

When the US developed the atomic bomb, it had an overwhelming military advantage over every other nation. So secret were the research and experimentation projects on nuclear weaponry that the expertise would have remained the west's sole property – had it not been for traitors like the Rosenbergs and Dr Klaus Fuchs.

The world has never been the same since an American scientist called Robert Oppenheimer led a dedicated band of researchers into the nuclear age. When the awesome fireball of nuclear fission exploded over the New Mexico desert on 16 July 1945 it could only be a matter of time before the harnessing of such energy would become the goal of dictators, tyrants and aspiring world-power players. The bomb was called Fat Boy and the mission to develop it The Manhattan Project. Ten miles from the Alamagordo Air Base, a complex of underground tunnels and bunkers, where much of the bomb's construction was carried out, was crammed with military top brass and civilian experts gathered to witness the greatest technological achievement ever reached by man. At 5.30a.m., in the cold morning drizzle, a ball of fire reaching 41,000 feet into the sky 12 feet higher than the tallest mountain, soared above the desert. The sound echoed like rolling thunder and the desert sand turned to glass in the 6,000 degree heat generated at the centre of the blast. Oppenheimer remembered at this incredible moment two verses from Sanskrit, the ancient language of India: 'If the radiance of a thousand suns were to burst into the sky, that would be the

A MISPLACED TRUST GAVE THE BLUEPRINTS FOR THE BOMB TO STALIN AND SET THE STAGE FOR DECADES OF FEAR

Below: ***Josef Stalin, Soviet dictator, was determined to harness the technology for the atomic bomb.***

splendour of the mighty one. I am become death – that shatterer of worlds'.

Every bomb, every missile, every rocket and explosive charge created since man first fashioned material for his wars was suddenly redundant. Oppenheimer hoped that the nuclear power he had developed would be turned into peaceful uses for the benefit of mankind. He knew that the war against Japan was going to be settled with his creation, but hoped in his heart that it would be so terrible in its destruction that no ruler would ever dream of using it again. For the American government, it was imperative that no government that was hostile to it would ever be given the chance. During wartime the technology for the production of the bomb was denied to the Germans and the Japanese, the Axis powers whose overthrow was imperative to the continuation of the democracies of the free world. After the war it was the Soviet Union that became the ideological enemy of America. At all costs it had to be denied access to both the material and the expertise necessary to construct an atom bomb. But the Soviet Union was to enter the nuclear race — and thus begin the Cold War – thanks to the betrayal of a brilliant scientist called Dr Klaus Fuchs. Fuchs came to Britain before the war from his native Germany, where he was a fugitive from Nazism. His intellect was put to use at Harwell, the government's top research centre where Britain was developing its own atomic programme. Everyone trusted the quiet, bespectacled don, who had signed the Official Secrets Act and who was deemed to be eternally grateful for sanctuary in his adopted country. It was a misplaced trust which gave the blueprints for the bomb to Stalin and set the stage for decades of fear, mistrust and confrontation between the world superpowers.

THE SOCIALIST SCHOLAR

Klaus Fuchs came from a long-line of Protestant pastors in Germany, socialist in outlook and beliefs. His father Emil raised his children to believe that the Soviet Union was the future and the salvation of the working man and that Nazism was to be resisted at all costs. In their hometown of Kiel the family were often ridiculed by right-wing newspapers for their convictions. Born in December 1911, he grew up in the shattered remnants of old Germany as first revolution, then inflation and finally the shadow of Nazism stretched over the country. A brilliant scholar, Klaus studied in Berlin, but his classes were soon to take second place to the priority of staying alive. The Gestapo had him and other family members at the top of their wanted lists because of his membership of the communist party and close links with Moscow. The communists smuggled him out of Germany in July 1933, first to Paris and then to London – a destitute refugee carrying everything he owned in a canvas bag.

Communism in pre-war England did not carry the bogeyman tag that it acquired after the conflict had ended. In fact his membership proved to the British government that he was a political asset in the resistance to Nazism and Fascism, which were spreading like a cancer across the face of Europe. MI5 and MI6 were aware of his communist past and reports noting it were filed in Whitehall. But he was never considered a security risk when, in 1934, he obtained a student internship under the physics professor Neville Mott at Bristol University. Mott later said of him: 'I had no qualms about him being a communist. Anyone who was against the Nazis probably was anyway. He seemed to know his stuff so I took him on and he produced some excellent work.

'He was shy and reserved and I can never remember discussing politics with him'. But politics were the engine of Klaus Fuchs. Although he had been given sanctuary in Britain, was learning there, being supported and sheltered there, the reality was that he despised the old order of the British Empire and its colonialism as much as he despised Nazism. From those earliest days there was only one true God that he worshipped, and it lived in the Kremlin and was called Josef Stalin.

Fuchs completed his doctorate at Bristol in 1936 and obtained a post-doctorate position at the laboratory of Max Born in Edinburgh. He never obtained British citizenship and found himself in the position upon the commencement of hostilities of being an enemy alien. He was placed in an internment camp on the Isle of Man, later being sent on to a camp with appallingly primitive conditions for the inmates in Quebec, Canada. Thanks to lobbying in high places by the friends he had made in academia he arrived back in Britain in December 1940, a free man. But there was a price for his freedom extracted by the government – harnessing his knowledge to the A-bomb programme that was underway. The physics community in Britain had a great wealth of talent to draw on as Hitlerism made fugitives of some of the greatest scientific minds of Europe. Klaus Fuchs was to be a cog in the great machine that would work on the greatest scientific project of all history.

Fuchs, with all his avowed history of communism, was allowed to sign the Official Secrets Act to be given clearance to work at the highest levels on the British atomic bomb. He worked on hideously complex mathematical problems for 'Tube Alloys,' one of the code names given to the project, and spent upwards of 16 hours a

Above and Below: ***The youthful Klaus Fuchs and the War Office in London, where his security clearance was processed.***

day trying to bring the theories of nuclear fission to reality in a secure laboratory at Birmingham University. In his off time he was a quiet man who rarely spoke unless asked a direct question, one who shunned the convivial company of his colleagues in a drink or a sporting event.

In 1941 he finally obtained British citizenship – just at the time that Hitler's hordes had launched their all-out assault on the Soviet Union. Fuchs was devastated at the news; he sincerely believed that if the communist state should fall it would be the end of civilisation as we knew it. It was after the launch of the invasion of Russia that Klaus Fuchs decided that the only way he could help the country he loved would be to pass on the secrets he had learned of the A-bomb. He had pledged 'to bear true allegiance to the Crown' at the ceremony where he became a British subject, but it was all so much talk to him; he planned to pass on everything he could to his Kremlin idols.

A DANGEROUS MEMORY

As part of his work he was allowed to read classified documents submitted by American scientists working on the development of the bomb. Fuchs was possessed of a phenomenal photographic memory which allowed him to absorb huge quantities of information merely at the glance of a page. It was a talent that would serve him well.

Fuchs' contact with the Soviet Union was Ursula Kuczynski, sister of Jurgen Kuczynski, a German who had been a member of the same anti-Nazi group which Fuchs had belonged to before fleeing the country. She was an agent with the GRU, the forerunner of the KGB, who Fuchs only knew as 'the girl from Banbury.' She was a Mata Hari of considerable skill and cunning, an operative who had served in China, Poland and Switzerland before being assigned to Britain. She and Fuchs were both controlled by a man named 'Alexander' who was a colonel in Red Army military intelligence whose real name was Kremer. Fuchs first hawked the knowledge that he had in his head by visiting the Soviet Embassy in London and offering details of the 'amazing project' that Britain and America were working on.

Sonia lived in Oxford, Fuchs was working in Birmingham so Banbury became the rendezvous where the secrets of the A-bomb were passed on. Fuchs often gave her written reports and she would transmit them to Moscow using the radio which she hid in one of her children's soft toys. If the reports were mostly mathematical they were sent via the diplomatic pouch between the Soviet Embassy in London and the Kremlin. Fuchs would later say: 'I passed her all the information I had. Since that time I had continuous contact with persons who were completely unknown to me, except that I knew that they would hand whatever information I gave them to the Russian authorities. I used my Marxist philosophy to establish two separate compartments in my mind. The first compartment contained friendships, personal relations, and the behaviour of the kind of man I wanted to be. The second compartment contained the dialectical necessity of correct party behaviour, espionage in the name of historical determinism, which gave me a peculiar sense of being a free man who could be completely independent of the surrounding forces of society. Looking back on it now, the best way of expressing it seems to be to call it a controlled schizophrenia'.

Above: ***He was almost anonymous in his civil service suit and hat, but Fuchs was the Kremlin's puppet.***

Opposite Top: ***The Los Alamos administration building in the New Mexico desert, where America's atom bombs were developed.***

Opposite Bottom: ***The destruction wrought by the second A-bombing of Japan, this one fell on the industrial city of Nagasaki.***

FUCHS' PHENOMENAL PHOTOGRAPHIC MEMORY ALLOWED HIM TO ABSORB HUGE QUANTITIES OF SECRET INFORMATION

Fuchs had passed on much that was crucial to the Soviet atom programme – but the real treasure trove of information lay in the US. His access to these secrets came in 1943 when he went to America as part of the British mission seconded under conditions of the strictest secrecy to the Manhattan Project, the code name for the development of the bomb. Here Sonia arranged for a man code-named Raymond to become his link with the Kremlin – Raymond later being exposed as the flamboyant and successful spy Harry Gold. Fuchs was assigned to work at the Oak Ridge gaseous diffusion plant for the production of fissionable uranium. Almost immediately he was passing on to his spymasters massive quantities of crucial information.

THE CENTRE OF POWER

On 14 August 1944 he moved to Los Alamos, the desert town in New Mexico which had been completely taken over by the military and sealed to the outside world. This was the inner sanctum, the holiest of holy sites in the charge to develop the atom bomb. Here under the direction of Oppenheimer the greatest physics brains in the world toiled towards their single goal of fissionable nuclear material with the explosive power of thousands of tons of TNT in a bomb no bigger than a refrigerator. In his book Klaus Fuchs: Atom Spy, author Robert Chadwell Williams wrote: 'For Fuchs, the transfer to Los Alamos was a golden opportunity, of which he took full advantage. The British Mission scientists, who were allowed access to many different divisions of the Manhattan Project, often had a better overview of the research than the Americans, who for security reasons were more compartmentalised. The British group made major contributions to the project, particularly in theoretical areas. Everybody knew Fuchs but few knew anything about him. Oppenheimer saw him as a man who seemed to be carrying the world's burdens on his shoulders. No-one seemed to perceive Fuchs as a security risk. To the other scientists he was simply a quiet German bachelor'.

In February 1945 Fuchs visited his sister, who had also escaped to England from Germany, at her home in Cambridge. En route he stopped to meet his contact Raymond in New York where he handed over considerable written accounts about the development of the plutonium bomb. At the meeting Fuchs explained he would probably be unable to meet Raymond for another year. The spymaster offered Fuchs $1,500 for expenses, a not inconsiderable sum. But Fuchs, the idealist, turned his nose up at the capitalist offering. 'I do not do this for the money', he told him. 'I do it because it is right. Because the only hope for mankind lies in communism'.

THERE WAS A FIVE-MONTH MI5 CHECK INSTITUTED ON FUCHS AFTER HIS COMMUNIST PAST RESURFACED

In fact Fuchs was able to get away from the tight security surrounding Los Alamos in June 1945, driving his battered blue Buick car to Santa Fe to meet Raymond as planned. This time the package contained full details of the plutonium bomb that was to be detonated at Alamagordo and the one that was to be dropped last on Nagasaki, the second Japanese city after Hiroshima to be destroyed with a nuclear weapon. He gave Raymond details of the test date and site – and just as importantly, the fact that America was indeed intending to end the war in the Pacific with the use of the weapon against Japan. Fuchs spent the next several months gleaning expert data on the production rate of uranium 235, plutonium and the necessary metal processes needed to keep fission safe before detonation. He handed them over to Raymond in September 1945, after which the two Japanese cities lay in ruins and mankind had awakened to the atomic age.

FUCHS DEVELOPED A CONSCIENCE WHEN HE SAW STALIN'S ACTIONS – BUT IT WAS TOO LATE TO STAVE OFF THE COLD WAR

Fuchs returned to England in the summer of 1946. After spending some time with his family he was absorbed as the leading physicist in the British bomb programme at Harwell, an RAF base on the Berkshire Downs a few miles south of Oxford. The target date for the bomb was set at 1952 and Klaus Fuchs was named as the Head of the Theoretical Physics Division and Deputy Chief Scientific Officer. Fuchs by this time had become an expert on other areas of nuclear power and wrote a landmark paper on fast reactors, predicting that all power stations in Britain would be using nuclear fuel by the 1980s. There was a five-month MI5 check instituted on Fuchs after his communist past resurfaced during a routine security scan, but nothing was ever done to replace him. His clearance by the intelligence community came at a time when new British prime minister Clement Attlee swore that all communist or fascist sympathisers found in a government post involving national security would be sacked.

Below: ***The nuclear desert left behind after the Hiroshima detonation.***

THE SPYING LIFE

His spying activities continued. He dropped information to couriers at London tube stations and at suburban pubs. He passed on details of the atom bomb tests on the Bikini Atoll and on British plutonium production. But there was something uneasy troubling his compartmentalised mind. As a highly intelligent human being he was having more and more trouble reconciling some of the more grotesque behaviour of the Soviet dictator Stalin with the glories of world communism. He later admitted: 'I knew I disapproved of a great many actions of the Russian government and the communist party'. He missed an appointment with his courier in 1949 and then decided not to keep another rendezvous as he wrestled with the demons of right and wrong. Klaus Fuchs had developed a conscience – but it was too late to stave off the start of the Cold War.

Fuchs was unmasked in December 1949. On the 29th of that month he celebrated his 38th birthday with friends at Harwell, displaying no outward signs of the inner torment which had racked him for the past several months. But those same friends who served him cake and coffee had no idea that just eight days previously Fuchs had been interviewed at Scotland Yard by MI5 intelligence officer William Skardon,

Left: ***The Energy Research Station at Harwell where Fuchs worked on the British bomb.***

FUCHS FINALLY CAME CLEAN WITH A CONFESSION THAT HE HAD COOLLY AND CALMLY GIVEN SECRETS TO THE SOVIET UNION

who told him that he was under suspicion as a man who had passed on nuclear secrets to the Russians. Skardon had no evidence and no powers of arrest – the point of the exercise was to try to get him to confess to his crimes. Fuchs denied the accusation while his mind raced as to who might have betrayed him. He also gave Skardon an insight into the way his mind worked when it came to loyalties. Fuchs claimed he was a loyal citizen of Britain, but that he reserved the right to 'act in accordance with my own conscience' if circumstances should arise in Britain similar to those which forced his exodus from Germany in 1933.

On 30 December Skardon arrived at Harwell and spoke with Harwell director Sir John Cockcroft. Cockcroft was told that Fuchs' father Emil had taken a university post in East Germany; that Klaus could be compromised as a major security risk because of it. Cockcroft demanded Fuchs' resignation ten days later and received it. Three days later Fuchs met with Skardon again and finally came clean with a detailed

Below: ***Sir Roger Cockroft, seated far right, talks to his research staff at Harwell. Fuchs is standing far left.***

detailed confession that he had coolly and calmly given the nuclear secrets of Britain and America ever since 1942 to the Soviet Union. On 30 January he travelled to the War Office where the statement was formalised and he was placed under arrest for treason. In it Fuchs said: 'At first I thought that all I would do would be to inform the Russian authorities that work upon the atom bomb was going on. They wished to have more details and I agreed to supply them. I concentrated at first mainly on the products of my own work, but in particular in Los Alamos I did what I consider to be the worst I have done, namely to give information about the principles of the design of the plutonium bomb. Before I joined the project most of the British people with whom I had made personal contacts were left wing, and affected, to some degree or other, by the same kind of philosophy. Since coming to Harwell I have met many English people of all kinds, and I have come to see in many of them a deep-rooted firmness which enables them to lead a decent way of life. I don't know where this springs from and I don't think they do, but it is there'. It later transpired that Fuchs had come under suspicion of the spycatchers because of his own actions.

SPYCATCHER SUPREME

Skardon, the government's chief spycatcher, was alerted to Fuchs by one Henry Arnold. In October 1949 Fuchs had gone to Arnold – the security officer at Harwell – and spoken with him about his father's appointment in East Germany, posing the question whether he should resign or not. Arnold, a personal friend, offered no advice but asked Fuchs what he would do in the eventuality of Soviet agents putting pressure on him. Fuchs replied that he really did not know. Such wavering put the seal on his fate as a spy. Arnold put duty above friendship and alerted MI5. The agency was already looking for a mole as spy activity both in Britain and America was suspected due to intelligence leaks from Soviet moles and 'turned' agents from behind the Iron Curtain. Later it was learned that FBI director J. Edgar Hoover took credit for stumbling upon the trail of a British spy, although that has never been precisely proved.

THE NEWSPAPERS EXPLODED WITH WHAT SEEMED THE FORCE OF AN A-BOMB AS THEY TOLD OF HIS TREACHERY

Signed copies of his confession were sent to the Attorney General who authorised prosecution of Fuchs under the Official Secrets Act. Ironically, if the Soviet Union had been an enemy and not an ally of Britain during World War Two he could have been charged with treason – a capital offence – but as it was the charges would lead him to eventually receiving a long prison term.

It was finally to the Old Bailey that Klaus Fuchs' long spy career ended on 1 March 1950 when he appeared to plead guilty as charged. Before his court appearance the name Professor Fuchs had already become a household name in Britain and the rest of the world. The newspapers exploded with what seemed the force of an A-bomb as they chronicled his treachery over the years, finally asking the question that all free governments were asking themselves: just how much damage had Klaus Fuchs done with his misguided, idealistic, 'compartmentalised' code of ethics which told him that what he was doing was morally acceptable? The answer was, quite simply, enormous damage.

Above: ***Security officers from Harwell – Henry Arnold (right) and W.J. Skarden – arrive at the Old Bailey on 1 March 1950 for the start of the Fuchs trial.***

'YOU HAVE BETRAYED BRITISH PROTECTION WITH THE GROSSEST TREACHERY,' SAID LORD CHIEF JUSTICE GODDARD

His trial lasted just 90 minutes at the Number One Court – scene of so many trials of heinous criminals stretching back to wife killer Dr Crippen. Some 80 newsmen were present to hear the presiding Judge, Lord Chief Justice Goddard, tell the defendant that what he did bordered on high treason. 'You have betrayed British protection with the grossest treachery', he said, 'fol-

Left: ***The Old Bailey, London, where Fuchs was found guilty of spying.***

Below: ***The gaunt features of the convict after nine-and-a-half years in jail. He travelled to a hero's welcome in East Germany, his spiritual home.***

lowing the pernicious creed of communism. Your atomic espionage has done irreparable harm to both England and America. You have imperilled the right of asylum and liberty for other refugees from tyranny. Your crime is only thinly differentiated from high treason'. Without further ado he was sentenced to the maximum 14 years in jail and taken down to the cells below.

Evidence supplied in his confession helped the FBI to Harry Gold – Raymond – and a 30 year jail term for his activities. It also helped smash the Rosenberg spy ring, leading to the executions of Ethel and Julius Rosenberg in New York for their trade in nuclear secrets. But the damage had been done with the announcement of the Soviet Union early in the 1950s that it had exploded a nuclear bomb. The reckoning was that it had come seven to ten years before the expected time thanks to the treachery of Klaus Fuchs, the misguided zealot for communism.

A SCHOLARLY PRISONER

He served nine years in jail, sewing mailbags and reading great tomes of Russian literature from the prison library in between organising physics classes for his cellmates. The graduates of the school of armed robbery and burglary suddenly found themselves being taught about neutrons and nuclei by one of the most distinguished minds of the age. While he was inside he was racked by fear that when his sentence was up the British would send him to America for trial, where he may have been sentenced to death as the post-war communist witch hunts were reaching fever pitch. Instead, his father Emil managed to convince the guardians of the East German state that he deserved a place there and it was granted. The British released him early and he was delighted that he was not to be deported to America. He flew to East Berlin as Mr Strauss aboard a Polish Convair plane. At Heathrow Airport he said: 'I bear no resentment whatsoever about Britain. In a way I'm sorry to be leaving'. He lived outside Dresden, becoming director of the country's nuclear physics programme. Apparently, he was rarely troubled that he had sold the nation which had sheltered him from the Gestapo down the river.

PAUL VICKERS
The Lust Murder

There didn't seem to be a lot lacking in the life of successful surgeon Dr Paul Vickers. He was widely recognised as an expert in his field by his fellow practitioners. However, his relationship with his wife was poor and would end in tragedy.

Dr Paul Vickers was a brilliant surgeon who rose to the very top of his chosen profession. He was also active in the British Medical Association, the governing body for practitioners and their policy, a position which required him to travel to conferences both at home and abroad. The trips were more than just business affairs for Vickers; they became personal escapes from the routine of his home life. At 42, he was locked in an unhappy marriage with his wife Margaret, a woman he had met while studying medicine at Cambridge. During the undergraduate years there Margaret had a reputation of being a social butterfly, a life and soul of the party type who had a ready smile, eager charm and a razor sharp wit. If anything, she was more academically qualified than her suitor, who struggled in his examinations. But they fell in love and married and shortly afterwards she gave birth to their only child, a son they named John. As is often the case in marriage Margaret had to compromise her own career – which looked to be promising – for the sake of her husband and child. But this self-denial seemed to trigger in her a cancer of hatred, of bitterness. When they moved to Gosforth-on-Tyne, to be near his appointment at the Queen Elizabeth Hospital in Gateshead, she went with reluctance. Soon the house was run down, she was moody, the garden was untended and there were constant rows between them. No wonder Vickers relished his trips away, trips where he could meet beautiful women, drink fine

THE HOUSE WAS RUN DOWN, SHE WAS MOODY, THE GARDEN WAS UNTENDED AND THERE WERE CONSTANT ROWS

Opposite: ***Respected, comfortable and secure – many men would have envied Dr Paul Vickers his lot in life.***

Below: ***Margaret and Paul Vickers on their wedding day. They seemed to be perfectly matched.***

AT 29, PAMELA WAS 13 YEARS HIS JUNIOR. SHE LED HIM TO HIS DOOM LIKE A MERMAID LEADING SAILORS ON TO ROCKS

Right: ***An anonymous house in an anonymous road. No-one had any idea of the nefarious activities going on inside.***

Below: ***The death certificate for Margaret Vickers. Her scheming husband thought that he had got away the perfect murder.***

wine and forget for a few days at least the torment of life with Margaret and her ever-deepening depression.

There was one women he met in 1976, in Brussels, that would change his life forever. She was called Pamela Collison, then, at 29, 13 years his junior, and her sexy allure led him to his doom like a mermaid luring sailors on to the rocks. Pamela was a tall, cool, leggy brunette who liked to wear fish-net stockings and Janet Reger silk under-wear beneath slinky, figure-hugging cock-tail dresses. She worked by day as a political research assistant – hence her appearance at the medical conference in Belgium – and indeed would go on to work briefly for Mr Michael Heseltine when he was Minister for the Environment. But by night she liked to party. From the moment he saw her, Dr Vickers was hooked. She was sensual, she was beautiful – and,most importantly, she seemed to be interested in him. He was balding, paunchy around the middle, saggy in the face, and yet seemed to have a magnetism of his own. Later, after his lust for Pamela had destroyed him completely, various friends stepped forward with stories of how he could turn on the charm for the ladies. Alastair MacFarlane, who had known him since their student days, said: 'Paul dressed smartly, was a good talker, but I just can't say why they went out with him or why they stayed with him. He had something I suppose, but I don't quite know what it was'. To someone like Pamela he represented a good 'catch' if he ever chose to leave his wife. He harboured ambitions to become a member of the European Parliament and spoke to her over drinks in Brussels of various money-making schemes he had. They shared conversation and a meal, but the relationship remained platonic. It was when they were both back in England that Vickers realised he was having great difficulty in getting the thought of the alluring Miss Collison out of his head.

D. Cert.
S.R./R.B.D.

CERTIFIED COPY OF AN ENTRY
Pursuant to the Births and Deaths Registration Act 1953

DEATH — Entry No. 24

Registration district: Newcastle upon Tyne
Administrative area: Metropolitan District of Newcastle upon Tyne
Sub-district: Newcastle upon Tyne

1. Date and place of death: Fourteenth June 1979. Royal Victoria Infirmary, Newcastle
2. Name and surname: Margaret VICKERS
3. Sex: Female
4. Maiden surname of woman who has married: PROBERT
5. Date and place of birth: 2nd March 1936. Wales.
6. Occupation and usual address: Wife of Paul Richard James VICKERS. Surgeon. 16, [illegible] Crescent, Gosforth. Newcastle upon Tyne
7. (a) Name and surname of informant: Paul Richard James VICKERS
(b) Qualification: Widower of deceased
(c) Usual address: 16, [illegible] Crescent, Gosforth. Newcastle upon Tyne
8. Cause of death:
I (a) Cardio respiratory Arrest
(b) Septicaemia + Probable sub arachnoid haemorrhage.
(c) Aplastic Anaemia
Certified by S. J. Armstrong MB
9. I certify that the particulars given by me above are true to the best of my knowledge and belief: [illegible signature] Signature of informant
10. Date of registration: Eighteenth June 1979
11. Signature of registrar: [illegible] Registrar

Certified to be a true copy of an entry in a register in my custody.

THE CHEATING GAME

Dr Vickers was no stranger to the cheating game. When he had first married he had taken a mistress called Julie Heaton, a woman he met on a dance floor at a disco in Newcastle-upon-Tyne when he was a newly-qualified doctor. Schoolteacher Julie went with him to London, Dublin and Paris as his 'wife' as he told her tales of his real wife's mental illness. Another schoolteacher called Mary McNally also became his lover, offering him sex and sympathy as he poured his heart out about being trapped in a loveless marriage. Now Miss Collison became his magnificent obsession and he was determined to do anything to possess her. She lived in London, almost 300 miles from him, so he had to dream up a scheme to get to see her. For the first meeting he attended a medical meeting which in reality held no interest for him at all. But it allowed him to make that all-important first contact with Pamela. They dined at a Mayfair restaurant, sipping fine wine and brandies late into the night before he dropped her off in Knightsbridge. The next night he told her that he loved her and within a fortnight Dr Vickers had become Dr Jekyll and Mr Hyde – the family man in Gosforth during Monday to Friday, the adulterer with his mistress in London on weekends and holidays. Vickers felt elated – not just because he was bedding a beautiful, younger

THE Sun

Wednesday, October 8, 1980 12p TODAY'S TV: PAGES 14 and 15

DOCHERT IS SACKE —See Back Pa

Bank rate to be cut 2% next month

By WALTER TERRY

INTEREST rates are to be cut by two per cent next month, the Treasury has decided.

At last Chancellor Sir Geoffrey Howe is able to ease the pressure on industry and help make mortgages and bank borrowing cheaper.

ACCUSED

Surgeon and girl charged with murder of his wife

By DOUG WATSON and MIKE GAY

SURGEON Paul Vickers and his attractive former girlfriend, Pamela Collison, were charged early today with the murder of his wife.

The couple were driven from London to Tyneside where they will appear in court later today.

Mrs Margaret Vickers, a mathematician, died in hospital, aged 44, from what was diagnosed as a rare blood disease.

Mr Vickers, 45, is an internationally famous orthopaedic surgeon in charge of the accident department of the Queen Elizabeth Hospital, Gateshead, Tyne and Wear.

LEAVE

He took leave of absence when the police investigation began.

Mr Vickers has been away from his home at

Continued on Page Two

Former girlfriend Pamela Collison . . . she was once Environment Minister Michael Heseltine's secretary

JURY TOLD OF 'MASS MURDER CONTRACTS' Page Seven

woman, but because he felt that he was getting what he 'deserved' in life. A cruel streak in him led him to think that he had been cheated of what was rightfully his in his marriage to Margaret. Now he was making up for lost time.

In London there was no attempt at a cover-up – indeed, the newly-liberated surgeon flaunted his mistress like some badge of honour. He even began showing her off in the company of his distinguished med-

Above: The Sun*'s glaring headlines say it all.*

Left: *The toll begins to mount on Dr Vickers as evidence piles up against him.*

VICKERS WAS LIKE A LITTLE BOY LOST IN HIS FIRST INFATUATION. HE WORSHIPPED THE GROUND PAMELA WALKED ON

Below: ***Mrs Julie Heaton, one of the witnesses called in to give evidence in the case of the twisted surgeon.***

ical colleagues. Dr Gerard Vaughan, one of his associates, later spoke of the embarrassment that he felt when Vickers invited him out to lunch and he saw this unknown woman on his arm. 'He introduced her as someone who was making a study of medical politics', said Dr Vaughan. 'But she contributed nothing to the conversation on that subject. And I was embarrassed by his nod and wink manner of suggesting he had something going with her'. In fact, Pamela was not a woman that Paul Vickers could easily say no to. Forceful and determined in her outlook and temperament, it was she who insisted on going everywhere with him. Someone later commented that Vickers was like a little boy lost in his first infatuation. He worshipped the ground that Pamela walked on and showered her with expensive presents – bought from his not inconsiderable income. Much of the money was spent on her favourite passion – clothes – and she stocked her wardrobe with designer label garments which would one day be aired in a court of law and bring gasps of admiration and envy.

A DEPRESSING PICTURE

Dr Vickers told her that he never made love with his wife, that she was almost a vegetable with her depression. He painted to her a picture of someone who was almost incapable of looking after herself on a routine basis, someone for whom life was not worth living. But this was very far from the truth; although Margaret was a burden to him, she had plenty to live for. With encouragement, kindness, even fondness from her husband who had once pledged to care for her in sickness and in health, she could have made a complete recovery from her fits of depression. Paul Vickers, however, had no intention of ever trying to make a new start of his marriage; his all consuming passion now was Pamela Collison. She was a demanding woman, a woman who told him in no uncertain terms that she would never be content just to play the 'little woman' at home while he was out working. Social respectability and social climbing were the things that interested her and Dr Vickers pondered how best to go about attaining these twin goals for her.

She was thrilled for him when he sought out the patronage of the Tory party to stand as a Euro MP and serve in Brussels – the place where he had first met Pamela. But both he and she were devastated when four separate constituencies turned him down as 'unsuitable'. Tyneside Tory organiser Joan Reeve later said of him: 'From the first time I met him there was something about him which made me shudder. The girls in the office didn't like him either. They said he made their flesh creep'. It dawned on him that Pamela would forever remain 'unsuitable' in the eyes of those who blocked the pathway to promotion and social status while she remained his mistress. He thought about divorce, but was too scared and too much of an emotional coward to put himself and Margaret through such an ordeal. Soon the prospect of the perfect murder began to form in his scientific, calculating mind.

A DEADLY DRUG

Vickers got his mistress – without telling her what it was for – to collect from him on prescription a drug called CCNU. This was a chemotherapeutic cancer drug, used to treat cancerous cells in a body.

But like all cancer-attacking drugs, healthy cells are also killed. Quite simply put, if given to someone who doesn't have cancer, the extremely strong drug would attack the white cells in the bone marrow, killing off the life force which makes up much of the blood in the body. Soon enough white cells would be lost that the patient injected with CCNU would resemble a leukaemia victim.

This is what Paul Vickers, a man hitherto faithful to his Hippocratic Oath if not his marriage vows, was planning for Margaret. At first Margaret felt marvellous when he gave her the first capsule; new energy seemed to return to her and she was up out of bed, spring cleaning the house in a way in which she had not attempted for years. And then as soon as the initial effects of the drug had worn off she was overcome with a terrible lethargy; every bone in her body ached, she could no longer get up in the mornings, she was frequently sick and she needed naps at all times of the day.

Her 'caring' husband took her to the hospital where he worked and lied to a fellow doctor that she was taking no medication. Four weeks after she had taken the first dose she was sick enough to have all the symptoms of the advanced stages of leukaemia. Consultant Ronald Thompson took his colleague to one side and said: 'She has no chance of survival – you must prepare yourself for the worst'. The drug that he had

Above and Left: ***Two studies in how the law takes its toll. Pamela Collison remained breezy, aloof and distant during the trial. The same cannot be said for erstwhile lover.***

been feeding her had literally smashed her body's capability of regenerating white cells. Vickers showed no emotion when the consultant told him this – but his colleagues thought this was merely stoicism on the part of a man who had to mask his feelings in front of numerous relatives over the years when he had to tell them that death was about to claim one of their loved ones.

On the eve of their 17th wedding anniversary in June 1979, Margaret died. The callous Vickers had her buried in an unmarked plot at the local cemetery; he did not even want to shell out for a headstone in her memory. He was now free to marry Pamela Collison. But things didn't work out quite the way either of them had planned. Like thieves falling out over treasure, soon the arguments between Collison and Vickers grew worse. His Oscar-winning performance at faking grief over his wife's death had led her to believe that they would be walking up the aisle as man and wife together within months. But something snapped within Vickers; he realised that the wildcat lover that had aroused him and captivated him so fully was never going to make him happy in the role of a wife. Vickers believed he would be in for a lifetime of misery. Instead he dumped her amid cant, bitterness and hatred – and instead of a lifetime of unhappiness, he is left with a lifetime in prison. For when the affair ended the woman scorned went straight to the police with the tale of a dead wife, dangerous drugs obtained on prescriptions and the story of a torrid affair. But Pamela had walked into a dangerous area – for the police, while believing her

Above: ***Pamela Collison, with the smile of victory on her lips, after being sensationally freed at the end of her trial.***

Below: ***Michael Heseltine, for whom she once briefly worked.***

story, charged her with murder too. And for good measure she was charged with obtaining drugs by deception – the one charge she admitted to. Soon the British public were treated to the spectacle of one of the most sensational murder trials this century; only the third in which a doctor has stood accused of murder.

The trial at Teeside Crown Court in 1981 was judicial theatre of the highest order. Day after day the newspapermen in the court struggled to keep up with the machine-gun pace of allegation and counter-allegation in the proceedings. Vickers quickly emerged as a man totally besotted with Pamela Collison – and like thieves who have fallen out, he was quick to paint her as a scarlet woman who was not to be trusted.

DANGEROUS DRUGS

The court heard that Mrs Vickers was fed a total of 52 capsules of the cancer-fighting drug over an eight month period. The defence for Collison was that she knew she was supplying him with dangerous drugs, but that she believed it was for research purposes only. Vickers, a man full of venom, denied murdering his wife and was determined to drag the name of the woman who had shopped him to police through the mud. He claimed that on their first date she had stripped off her clothes in his hotel room and climbed into bed unasked next to him. He claimed that she told him 'of sexual relations with a great number of men, generally two at a time'. He claimed that she talked about whipping and bondage, 'and said that she was a mean hand with a whip'. He claimed that he swore he saw scars on her back caused by a whipping she had received from 'a distinguished academic'. He said that a cigarette burn on her cheek was the souvenir of a way-out bondage session with another man. She said he sent her pornographic pictures of herself which he kept hidden in his home to look at after he had finished work. He said she had been on the contraceptive pill since the age of 12, was raped three times and had contracted a venereal disease once.

He told the court that he had got the powerful drug on forged prescriptions to try to treat his wife not kill her. But soon he said she was using the prescriptions to try to blackmail him when he wanted to end the affair. He said he paid her £4,000 for work she did which would normally have not exceeded £1000. 'I had to keep seeing her because she was clearly a very disturbed person and I had a feeling of concern for her'. He said his problems were Collison's demands for more money to support her lavish lifestyle and more prescriptions. 'Most of all', he added, 'the CCNU which was arriving at my house in a far greater quantity that I could have wanted'. He then said wistfully: 'I think if two people were not meant to meet it was myself and Miss

Above: ***Mr Justice Boreham, who tried the Vickers case, sentenced the doctor to life and recommended that he serve a minimum of 17 years behind bars.***

VICKERS CLAIMED THAT COLLISON TALKED ABOUT WHIPPING AND BONDAGE 'AND SAID THAT SHE WAS A MEAN HAND WITH A WHIP'

Collison'. He went on to tell how he tried to 'ditch' Miss Collison by palming her off on to a friend at the hospital who he thought might like her company. He added: 'I have every considerable sympathy for her, but I think she's an extremely disturbed person, a relentless blackmailer. I was trying to keep the lid on her'. He said his feelings for her began to change after she attacked him with a knife when she saw a picture of him and his wife at a friend's flat in France. Collison's defence counsel Mr Robin Stewart QC said at one point: 'Isn't it true that there was a flaming row between you when she found out you were, and still were, a married man?' Vickers replied:

Above: ***Paul Vickers in the trademark pinstriped suit that he wore throughout the trial.***

Opposite Left and Right: ***Vickers tried to persuade the court that he had never plotted murder against his wife, but it was all to no avail.***

'That is total rot. She knew from the first time we had dinner in November 1977 that I was married and I reinforced it when she came into my hotel room'.

PRIVACY DISAPPEARS

Every shred of privacy and intimacy in the relationship was ripped away. The court heard how he called her 'Kitten Eyes' and in one sexy letter said: 'You must realise that I'll master you. If this is not what you want you had better retreat fast'. He saw vivacious Pam as the perfect woman – although a psychiatrist told the court that Vickers was really nothing better than a pathetic little boy. Psychiatrist Dr John Hawkins said: 'He had difficulty in striking up relationships with women. There is no doubt that his relationship with his wife was a disturbed one, probably dictated from childhood. He feels a need to dominate women. He is egocentric and pretends self-confidence to mask his insecurity'. But he said that he was certainly suitable to stand trial on the charge of murder.

Pamela maintained a discreet silence throughout the trial, content to keep the public amused and agog with her stunning array of outfits which she wore day after day. On the 19th day of the trial she held the court's attention completely as she read an 11-minute speech from the dock. She declined to go into the witness box, but exercised her right under British law to make a statement from the dock. Judge Mr Justice Boreham asked her to speak clearly and slowly so that he and a shorthand writer could take a full note of what she was to say. As she spoke her former lover sat slumped against the edge of the dock.

A PREPARED SPEECH

Reading from a large notepad Collison said: 'My lords, I have chosen to make a statement from the dock because there is very little I can add to what I told the police in May 1980. I do not wish to go into the details of the personal and intimate relationship with Mr Vickers. I am not guilty of the murder of Mrs Margaret Vickers. Neither have I been party to any plot to murder her. I cannot say what happened to any CCNU I sent to Mr Vickers. As I told the police, I had prescriptions dispensed for CCNU between September 1978 and December 1978. I have never asked Mr Vickers to provide me with any prescriptions for CCNU and I was never asked to obtain any after I stopped working in Central London since December 1978. Nor did I. No prescriptions were given to me in the name of Mrs Margaret Vickers and I had no idea whatsoever that the drug was for his wife's use. As I told the police, Mr Vickers told me that the drug was unavailable to him in Newcastle-upon-Tyne and he felt that was unfair because he wanted it for research trials. Perhaps I was stupid not to question him further, but I believed him to be acting correctly, being a prominent member of the British Medical Association and the

General Medical Council. I had no idea that the drug was to be used in any way other than was properly, medically directed.

'I have never blackmailed Mr Vickers in cash or kind and resent the attempt to besmirch my name and reputation, and the inference he draws from any relationships. I might have had thrush, which is a common complaint, but I have never had any venereal disease. The contraceptive pill was not available in 1959 when I was 12, as alleged by Mr. Vickers, and I did not take it until my early twenties. I am a pro-

fessional economist and statistician. All my relationships with Members of Parliament have been on a purely political basis. During the time I worked for Mr Michael Heseltine as his political research assistant there were no leaks or unauthorised contact with any member of the Press. I have never made any applications to the Criminal Injuries Compensation Board and have been neither raped nor mugged. I have no scars on my back or elsewhere, nor cigarette burns on my face. I have never threatened to spray paint on Mr Vickers' car or damage his home or property. I have had arguments and fights with him, especially after discovering his marriage. I have never attacked him with any weapon nor terrorised him in any way. The letters I received from Mr Vickers I regarded as nothing more than love letters, and never thought there was anything sinister in them, and still don't. I thought he was seeing his solicitor about his divorce and that is what I assumed many of the references to mean. I only discovered he was married after we had been going out together for five months and I agreed to act as his research assistant for the European Parliamentary Elections. In fact I never met, saw or spoke to Mrs Vickers. Mr Vickers explained to me that his wife was a schizophrenic and had been confined to a mental hospital since the birth of their son. He later told me that divorce proceedings were under way, and I had no idea at the time that he lived with his wife.

COMMUNICATION BREAKDOWN

'Mr Vickers accompanied me to many dinners, conferences and parties. He introduced me to many members of the BMA Executive. In November 1979 I believed I was pregnant and this appeared to be confirmed by my temperature charts. Mr Vickers was in one of his fits of isolationism and I tried to contact his local curate to bring about some form of communication between us. Towards the end of November 1979 we agreed to get married and in early December I made provisional arrangements in London. I then discovered I was not pregnant and so, because of his eccentric behaviour, I cancelled the Register Office Booking. During late November his behaviour became increasingly peculiar. He

Opposite: ***The end for Vickers as he is driven away with the judge's life sentence ringing in his ears.***

Left: ***Vickers was facing life in jail, but the mistress with whom he had shared good times was free.***

Below: The Sun*'s headline showed that while Collison was free, she still earned the scorn of many.*

wife, and when in particular the killing is achieved not in a moment of passion but by a process which was cruel, insidious and slowly deliberate and then fatal, then in my judgement inhumanity has plunged to the very depths. The case against you is overwhelming'.He sentenced him to life imprisonment with a recommendation that he serve a minimum of 17 years. Collison was given a six month jail sentence, suspended for two years, for obtaining the murder drug illegally for him.

In 1983 his leave to appeal against the conviction was refused as the evidence against him was declared by Law Lords to be 'overwhelming'.

THE Sun

Saturday, November 21, 1981 12p SPORT STARTS ON PAGE 24

CROWD JEERS TH
MISTRESS AS DR
DEATH GETS LIFE

'SLUT' FURY OVER FREED PAM

Battling through the mob . . . police escorting Pamela to her car after she was cleared of murder yesterday

Picture by KEITH PERRY

'When a man whose vocation is to alleviate pain kills so cruelly and slowly, then inhumanity has dropped to the very depths'

MR JUSTICE BOREHAM

By DOUGLAS WATSON and MICHAEL GAY

FREED mistress Pamela Collison ran a gauntlet of fury last night.

A 200-strong mob screamed "slut" at her after her ex-lover was jailed for life for murdering his wife.

The crowd hissed and booed as Miss Collison, a 34-year-old blonde, was bundled into a car by police.

DRUG

She had been cleared of murder by the "passion and poison" trial jury.

But the judge at Teesside Crown Court, Mr Justice Boreham, said surgeon Paul Vickers should serve at least 17 years for slowly poisoning his wife Margaret with the powerful anti-cancer drug CCNU.

He grimly told the death-dealing doctor:

'To judges it is no unfamiliar thing to have to witness what might be called man's inhumanity to man. But when a medical practitioner whose vocation is clearly to alleviate pain and suffering deliberately kills, this, even for a judge, is a new field.

And when, as here, the victim was your wife and when in particular the killing is achieved not in a moment of passion but by a process which was cruel, insidious and slowly deliberate and then fatal, then in my judgment inhumanity has plunged to the very depths.'

DR JEKYLL'S SORDID SECRETS: Pages 2 & 3 ● RIDDLE OF PAMELA'S POLITICIAN LOVER: Page 4

TEARS

Vickers, 47, showed no sign of emotion as he was led away, after bowing to the judge.

But Mss Collison left the dock in tears after the Not Guilty ver-

Continued on Page Three

accused me of bizarre things, such as mounting a campaign to remove him from the General Council and he told me on several occasions to commit suicide. I am not guilty of the murder of Mrs Vickers. I have never had any wish to harm her nor have I conspired to bring about her death'.

The trial last for 25 days in all and soon it became clear that Collison had nothing to do with the murder of Mrs Vickers. It had been carried out solely by Vickers, even though Collison had broken the law by cashing in the forged prescriptions he wrote for the drug. The jury took five hours after being sent away by the judge to reach their unanimous verdict of guilty on Vickers. They came back 20 minutes later with acquittal for Collison. Then Vickers was ordered to stand and face the wrath of the judge who told him: 'To judges it is no unfamiliar thing to witness what might be called man's inhumanity to man. But when a medical practitioner, whose vocation is clearly to alleviate pain and suffering, deliberately kills, this – even for a judge – is a new field. And when, as here, the victim was your

ANGELO/ALLITT
Angels of Death

There are few nightmares that terrorise the entire population more than that of killer nurses. When the image of those who are normally associated with kindness and caring is tarnished by individuals who abuse the trust placed in them, society trembles.

All Richard Angelo wanted to be in life was the good guy – the hero who earned the praise and admiration of his fellow man. Throughout his childhood he was the quiet kid in school who got bullied, the nonentity who could never compensate for lack of friends by winning praise from his teachers. Angelo was an only child who turned to his father for solace and friendship, accompanying him on fishing and hunting expeditions.

As an awkward young man, it was the same story with him. Friends were something that other people had. And respect was a commodity that did not figure highly in his existence. Until the day when he became a nurse and realised that he had the power to give life.

Or death – and it was through the latter that this grey, soulless individual, struggling for recognition in a world that he believed was against him, found the fleeting moments of heroism and respect. As a respected emergency medical technician at a hospital near New York he found the answer to his mediocrity – and four people died because of it. Angelo injected the patients in his care with a muscle relaxant that triggered heart spasms and breathing constrictions. Then, as death seemed about to take his patients, he would rush in, frenzied, authoritative, in control – appearing as a life-giver in a critical situation. The true hero.

But while he pulled off 27 such miracles of medicine, four people died agonising deaths – innocent people who had entrusted themselves to his care, believing that he was a dedicated professional. It was a case that rocked America to its very core and led to more stringent control of such drugs in the hands of nurses like Angelo.

After he was caged for 50 years to life it was left for the relatives of the victims to mourn – and the psychiatrists and mind doctors to debate over where the first seeds of evil were planted in his humdrum life. 'How this God fearing altar boy grew up to become some crazed Frankenstein, performing these macabre and outrageous stunts to satisfy his own perverted ideas of self-worth, must, somewhere hold a salutary lesson for us all', said Dr James Cecilson, who has made a detailed study of the Angel of Death.

He, and others, say that to understand what made him do it it is necessary to look at his roots and comprehend how a desperately lonely boyhood would eventually force him to seek excitement in such a grotesque manner later in life. He was born in 1962 to teacher parents Joseph and Alice Angelo who raised him as a strict Catholic and doted on his every whim. He attended church every Sunday without fail in the small Long Island town of Lindenhurst and became known to one and all as Little Ricky. But Little Ricky didn't stay that way for long – too many sweet pastries eaten from the hand of his doting Italian grandfather turned him into a chubby child by the time he was five. Soon the taunts of 'fatso' and 'lardback' were burning into his psyche, devaluing his own currency of self-esteem like an acid scorching through metal. Instead of being able to taunt children back, he turned in on himself, devoting himself from the age of six onwards to the Our Lady of Perpetual Help Church where he was altar boy.

MUMMY'S BOY

He received a good education at the nearby Perpetual Help Elementary School and later at the St John the Baptist High School, but he was not a stunning pupil. Other children taunted him about his weight, about being a mummy's boy, about being generally stupid. He responded to this by growing closer still to his parents. Only in the goody two-shoes environment of the Boy Scouts did he seem to shine, as troop leader who won

THROUGHOUT HIS CHILDHOOD, ANGELO WAS THE QUIET KID IN SCHOOL WHO GOT BULLIED AND HAD NO FRIENDS

WHEN HE BECAME A NURSE HE REALISED HE COULD GIVE LIFE – IT WAS A WAY OF WINNING RESPECT AND FRIENDS

ANGELO WAS THE GOD-FEARING ALTAR BOY WHO GREW UP TO BECOME A KIND OF CRAZED FRANKENSTEIN

THE TAUNTS OF 'FATSO' AND 'LARDBACK' WERE BURNING INTO HIS PSYCHE, DEVALUING HIS SELF-ESTEEM

Opposite: ***Richard Angelo, the boy who craved recognition as a 'lifesaver' and a 'hero'. But his fleeting moments of heroism and respect cost many their lives.***

many badges. Here he was in his element – someone in charge of people, performing good deeds which he believed raised his worth in their eyes. The young hero.

When he was 17 he left high school and took a course in nursing at the State Agricultural and Technical College at Farmingdale where he seemed to have found his metier. He received good grades and was a diligent student. But while cordial to his classmates, he never joined in the usual high jinks of college, was never present at parties or other social events. Angelo buried himself in his scholar's books and seemed at peace with the world. In reality, the dark side within him was growing. Later, after his appalling crimes were uncovered, it was found that many of the books he took out of the medical library were concerned with poisons and potions – presumably he was boning up on the knowledge he would need to take life, not preserve it.

HE APPEARED TO BE A SERIOUS SCHOLAR, BUT MANY OF THE BOOKS HE STUDIED CONCERNED POISONS AND POTIONS

ANGELO WAS BONING UP ON THE KNOWLEDGE THAT HE WOULD NEED TO TAKE PEOPLE'S LIVES, NOT PRESERVE THEM

SOCIAL OUTCAST

After two years he graduated from college and took a job in the Burns Unit at the Nassau County Medical Centre. Here, in a day-to-day environment dealing with both patients and staff, he seemed to revert to his introverted old self and is not remembered fondly by his bosses. Hospital spokesman Edward Smith said: 'He was competent, but no more than that. He was in trouble with his fellow employees. He just couldn't get on with them. He was a social outcast, something of a pariah. He was always in trouble here and always calling in sick. He lasted for six months before resigning for "personal reasons". I understood that the personal reasons were that he wanted to go to Florida'.

In fact he went home and pondered his options for the future. He was unhappy at the hospital for a variety of reasons. Probably, deep down, he was unhappiest of all because he did not have access to drugs with which he could take life.

HE BECAME UNHAPPY BECAUSE HE DID NOT HAVE ACCESS TO THE DRUGS WITH WHICH HE COULD TAKE LIFE

After working for a year at the Brunswick Hospital in Amityville, he landed the job at the Good Samaritan Hospital in West Islip, Long Island, which would afford him the opportunities he needed for his berserk plan. Here the loner, the outcast, could achieve the attention he needed when he was appointed a member of the hospital's 'Code Blue' team. Code Blue is hospital argot used to summon the speediest of aid when a patient is dying. The innocent language is used over a hospital's loudspeaker system to avoid frightening relatives or visitors. Doctors, nurses and technicians who are part of the Code Blue team must abandon everything they are doing and rush to the designated spot to begin the battle to save a life.

ANGEL OF DEATH

A Code Blue at the Good Samaritan Hospital was sounded after heart, lung or other monitoring machines issue an alarm – or if a member of staff notices a patient in extreme distress. This was perfect for Angelo – at last he would be at the centre of attention, apparently a hero life-saver to his peers, while in actuality he was an angel of death. District Attorney John Collins, who was later to prosecute him, said: 'I don't think he cared one bit for the people he preyed upon. I think what all this was about was the emergency code and the rush of adrenalin it gave him. His was not the gratification of helping save life – his kick came in the taking of it. In other words, it is analagous to the fireman who sets the fire, and then sits there and watches it burn and then ultimately gets involved in fighting the fire. He doesn't give a damn whether the building ultimately burns down but that he was there to be seen fighting the fire...that he is seen as a hero'.

ANGELO WAS AT THE CENTRE OF ATTENTION, A HERO LIFE-SAVER TO HIS PEERS, BUT ACTUALLY AN ANGEL OF DEATH

In the last months of 1987 Richard Angelo treated the emergency rooms at Good Samaritan Hospital as his own personal playground of death. Using the drugs Pavulon and Anectine – paralysing drugs used as muscle relaxants – he could, in the right dosages, induce heart failure. In September of that year he worked in the combined cardiac-intensive care unit as an assistant supervisor, the perfect setting to play the hero – and have access to the drugs which enabled him to do it.

The first to die was John Fisher, aged 75, who was admitted on 4 September with signs of a stroke. By 7 September his condition had stabilised. But the following day he suffered a massive heart attack and died 20 minutes later. The next to die was Milton Poultney, 74, who was recovering from gall bladder surgery when he went into cardiac arrest on 16 September. He died hours later.

Next came Anthony Greene, 57, who suffered from a chronic chest disease. He was doing well until 28 September when he went into a respiratory coma. Although revived, he remained in a coma until he died on 16 October. Then on 9 October Frederick LaGois, aged 60, went into cardiac arrest the night before he was to undergo surgery. He died 12 hours later.

Losing patients in the high-stress, high stakes atmosphere of the emergency ward was nothing new. But no-one had ever had to work with the killer before. It would later transpire that the Code Blue leader – Angelo – had paid a quiet visit to the victims shortly before the alert was issued. And then he would reappear at the head of his team to become a lifesaver.

One man would fight back from the brink of death to give harrowing testimony at Angelo's trial. Gerolamo Kucich, 75, of Yugoslavia, who was visiting his son in America when he began to experience chest pains, found himself in the hospital under the watchful eye of Angelo. Early on the morning of 11 October a man wearing a white coat, who he thought was a doctor, came into his room and asked him how he was feeling before injecting something into his arm. These are the chilling words he related in court about how he felt at the time: 'A female nurse gave me a pill for pain in the morning. Then a man in a white coat appeared. He went right to the monitor and said: "Mr Kucich, how do you feel?" I said: "Not bad".

A NARROW ESCAPE

'The man opened his coat, pulled out what looked like a white fountain pen and said: "Now you are going to feel much, much better". I saw it was a needle. When he struck me I felt cold liquid. I was like dead. My muscles couldn't move. Everything went dead. The female nurse returned and I couldn't open my eyes. I heard her ask someone else in the room what he did and he said: "Nothing". I recognised the voice as that of the man who injected me. The woman was weeping and pleading with him to open my eyes. After a while, seconds or minutes that seemed like eternity, I heard her say: "He's started to breathe"'.

Above: ***A sad, confused childhood undoubtedly had its effect on Angelo's adult life.***

His co-workers began to call him the kiss-of-death because he was always present at so many tragedies. But they did not realise that their sick joke was true in every way. His berserk killing spree was only halted because Kucich made a complaint to police and they followed it up. When he was quizzed Angelo made no attempt at a cover up – even though he would later plead not guilty at his trial. In an 80-minute videotaped confession he said: 'I didn't want to hurt anybody. I did it to create crisis situations so that I would come out looking good'. Unmarked vials containing the drugs he used on his victims were discovered by detectives at his home, along with potassium chloride and hypodermic needles in his locker at work. 'I knew what I was doing and it was intentional',he said. 'The reason I injected it was because the unit was very busy and I felt inadequate in general. I felt I had to prove myself'.

CO-WORKERS BEGAN TO CALL HIM THE KISS-OF-DEATH BECAUSE HE WAS PRESENT AT SO MANY TRAGEDIES

He was found guilty at his trial in 1989 of murder, manslaughter and assault charge on at least six other patients who luckily survived. Superior Court Judge Alfred Tisch, sentencing him to spend 50 years to life in jail, said: 'You had no right to usurp

God's function. Each of those patients, in their way, had the right to enjoy every day that was available to them. In my 19 years on the bench I have heard many horror stories but the testimony of Mr Kucich is at the top of the list and gives a new meaning to the term "depraved indifference"'.

Angelo left the court to spend his days in a place where there aren't any heroes – only losers.

BEVERLY ALLITT

If Angelo was the worst nightmare for Americans, then his monstrous British equivalent must without doubt be Beverly Allitt. Her slaughter of the innocents in a hospital ward makes her Britain's worst female serial slayer – the crimes all the more horrifying because they were carried out against children. Allitt, 24, murdered or tried to murder seven babies and toddlers on her ward in a 59-day period. She also attacked six other small victims on Ward Four at Grantham Hospital during the same period, making her a woman more reviled in British society than Moors Murderess Myra Hindley.

Below: *Myra Hindley, the epitome of female evil – until the Beverly Allitt case.*

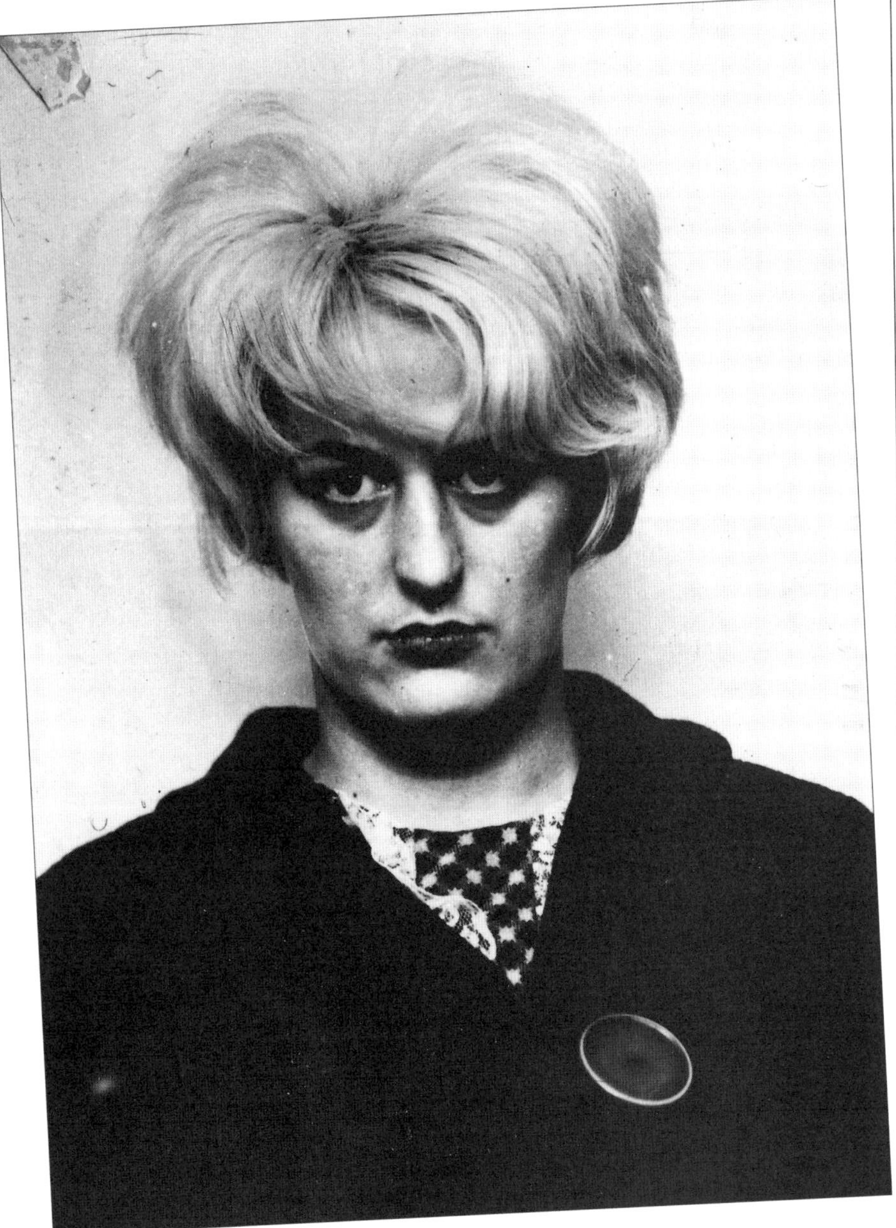

A sufferer of the rare syndrome 'Munchausen by Proxy,' Allitt could be a paragon of virtue and love one minute and ruthless killer the next. Munchausen's disease makes sufferers seek to draw attention to themselves by faking heart attacks or desperately injuring themselves. In Allitt's case it was by proxy – the harm was to others. Like Angelo, she craved attention and respect and so played the hero, trying to save the lives of the little ones whose lives she had initially placed in such mortal danger. Because her psychiatric disorder went unnoticed and untreated, she was able to roam about a National Health hospital like the grim reaper, gaining emotional satisfaction at the deaths of children.

DISTURBED CHILDHOOD

The sick hand that rocked the cradle of these doomed children was afflicted almost from birth. One of four children brought up in Corby Glen, a small Lincolnshire village, she was marked out from her earliest days as a child who craved attention. It would manifest itself in displays of tantrums, of dressing up, of talking loudly in class – anything which would ensure her more than a fleeting moment of acknowledgement from those in authority. Soon she took to going to school wearing plasters and bandages – but there were no wounds underneath. When that ruse was discovered she began bruising and cutting herself, proving to her peers and her teachers that she was genuinely hurt.

Her parents, Richard and Lillian, doted on her and believed her extreme methods to draw attention to herself were the product of nothing more than extreme enthusiasm. In fact, her self-esteem barely registered above zero – a precursor for Munchausen's Syndrome. Because she felt lost in the family, even though she was showered with affection, Allitt began to retreat into a make-believe world of wounds and illnesses by the time she was five years old, the world which would ensure that she was always the centre of attention. As she got older Beverly Allitt collected maladies the way some young teens collect boyfriends. There were stomach illnesses, urological illnesses, backaches, cramps, headaches and on and on.

A TRUSTED TEENAGER

At school she took CSE examinations and one O-level which she decided to eventually use towards a career in nursing. She had done a great amount of babysitting for friends as a teenager, a practice which earned her the respect and good wishes of all who trusted her. Her schoolfriend Rachel Oliver recalled: 'She did a lot of babysitting because she was very fond of children and seemed to have a knack of handling them. Even when she was very young she was always playing with her little brother, pulling him along in his pushchair. She was just great with kids'.

Allitt enrolled at Grantham College on a preparatory nursing course for two years and from there went to Grantham and Kesteven Hospital as a trainee. But although she passed her exams, she was the only student in her year not offered a full-time job because senior staff were worried about the extent of her sick leave. In one year alone she had 94 days off sick for her imagined illnesses. Between 1987 and 1991 she was treated at the hospital where she was training 24 times for broken bones, bruises, leg, back and head injuries – all of them self-inflicted wounds. In February 1991, however, she landed a six month contract to stay on at the hospital to work in the short-staffed children's ward. One detective would later say: 'It was a make or break period for her. She had been given the chance to shine and show she was a good nurse'. But strange demons in her warped personality were tugging at her. Her obsessive need for success, to be the centre of attention, was pulling at her already. The job which would give her power over life and death would ultimately tip her over the brink.

In 59 days in 1991 there were four deaths and numerous grievously hurt children. The first to die was Liam Taylor, eight weeks old, who suffered a mysterious heart attack on 23 February 1991. The boy, admitted for a chest infection, was given an insulin injection by Allitt as his parents slept in a hospital cot just feet away. Doctors switched off his life support machine and he died just a few hours later. The following victims are not in chronological order, but in order of the heinousness of the crimes.

Nine-week-old Becky Phillips was killed and her twin sister Katie was permanently brain damaged after two attempts to suffocate her. Peter Phillips and his wife Susan were emotionally devastated after the tragedies – but Allitt's demeanour was such that they believed her story that she had tried desperately to save Becky. They welcomed Allitt into their home and asked her to be godmother to Katie.

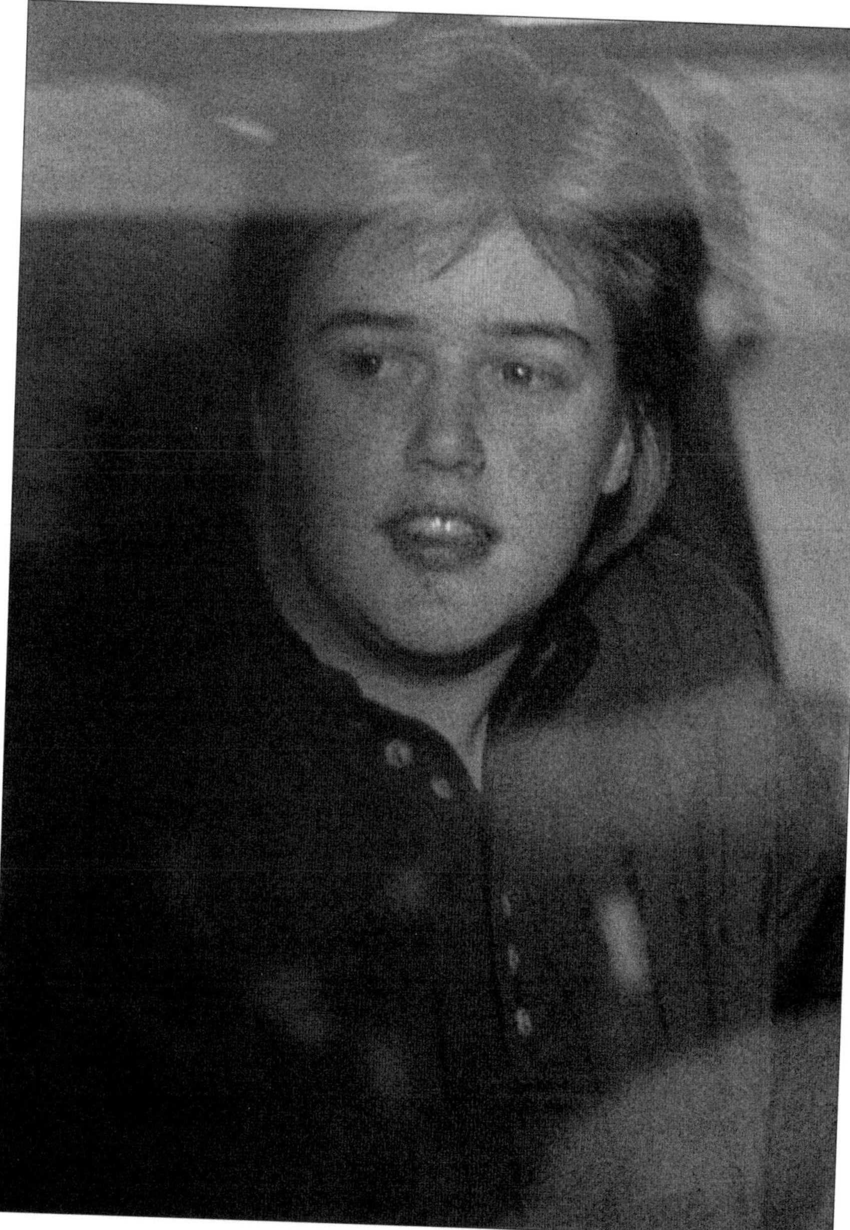

Above: ***Beverly Allitt is driven away from Grantham Magistrates Court after her first appearance there.***

'SHE DID A LOT OF BABYSITTING BECAUSE SHE WAS VERY FOND OF CHILDREN... SHE WAS JUST GREAT WITH KIDS'

Above: ***Superintendent Stuart Clifton of the Lincolnshire police force, who led the investigation into Allitt's crimes.***

WITHIN TEN MINUTES OF BEING LEFT ALONE WITH BEVERLY ALLITT, THE CHILD TURNED BLUE AND COLLAPSED

Becky and Katie had been born prematurely and were taken to the hospital for treatment for ailments – in Becky's case, an upset stomach. She was fed by Allitt and released – but her mother recalled the horror that confronted her in the night: 'Her eyes dropped to the bottom of their sockets. I thought I was seeing things but it happened again. Her face was twitching and then she started to cry. It was a pitiful screaming. I have never heard a cry like it before, nor have I heard it since'. The family GP was called but found both heartbeat and temperature normal. The couple took Becky to bed with them but two hours later she stopped breathing. They rushed her to hospital where she was found to be dead upon arrival. Only later was the cause of her death discovered – a massive dose of insulin.

Katie was declared healthy but doctors decided to run a series of tests on her. The nurse left in charge was – Beverly Allitt. Within ten minutes of being left alone with the child she had turned blue and collapsed. She collapsed again two days later and was rushed to a specialist baby unit at Nottingham City Hospital before being released back on to Ward Four of the Grantham Hospital and once again prey to the tender mercies of Nurse Allitt. As a result the child has cerebral palsy, permanent brain damage, it is unlikely that she will ever be able to walk unaided, she is partially blind and she will never be able to speak properly.

UNEXPLAINED DEATHS

Timothy Hardwicke, 11, was physically and mentally disabled when he was admitted to the hospital. He died three hours later from a heart attack. Kayley Desmond, 14 months old, was admitted with a chest infection. A week later she collapsed after her skin became mottled and breathing became much harder. Luckily she was transferred to a hospital in Nottingham where she recovered. The next victim, Paul Crampton, survived Allitt's unique brand of medicine – but only just. The five-month-old boy received the second highest dose of insulin ever recorded in the British Isles. He was later found to have had 43,147 milli-units of insulin for every litre of his blood when the normal level would have been 12 to 15 milli-units. The only higher reading ever recorded was on an adult doctor who committed suicide by injecting himself with the drug. Ironically, Paul was recovering from his chest infection when he was admitted because Allitt was off, but he deteriorated upon her return. He too was transferred to the hospital in Nottingham where he made good progress away from her ministrations.

Clare Peck was the fourth murder victim. Aged 15 months, she was admitted for treatment for asthma and was briefly alone with Allitt. Later she was found blue and not breathing. She recovered – but collapsed again when Allitt was alone with her again and doctors could not save her.

As a mood of despondency and grief swept the hospital the unexplained collapses continued. People blamed the air conditioning system, believing that Legionnaire's Disease may have broken out. They blamed mysterious viruses and unclean air filters. In fact they blamed everything, except the 13-stone nurse who always seemed to be around when disaster and tragedy struck. No-one as yet believed the children were victims of anything other than cruel fate, except for Paul Crampton, whose insulin reading was triggering alarm bells among hospital management.

The mysterious tragedies continued. Bradley Gibson, five, was admitted with pneumonia and had a heart attack shortly after Allitt started her shift. It took doctors 32 minutes to restore the five-year-old's heartbeat, but he was left disabled. Yik Hung Chan, aged two, fractured his skull in a fall and was admitted on to Ward Four. He was found dark blue and not breathing after Allitt attended to him. He was transferred to Nottingham where he recovered. Michael Davidson, aged seven, was admitted after being shot in an air-gun accident. Allitt was alone with him when his heart stopped. An emergency team saved Michael with seconds to spare.

FIGHTING FOR LIFE

Christopher Peasgood, eight months, was in an oxygen tent with a breathing alarm when it sounded. A nurse found him dark blue and arching his back. Allitt stood nearby. After he recovered she was assigned to look after him again – and he collapsed again. He recovered at Nottingham. Christopher King, nine months, was admitted with severe vomiting. Allitt was again alone with him when he turned a mottled blue colour. Doctors believed he would die but he, too, recovered at the hospital in Nottingham. Patrick Elstone was seven weeks old when he was admitted with an ear infection. He stopped breathing and went blue. His breathing alarm was turned off. Later Beverly Allitt was found guilty of causing him grievous bodily harm. He has been left permanently brain damaged.

In less than two months she had reaped a grim harvest, but it had thankfully come to an end. Police were working on the case when they received information from Dr Derrick Teale, a biochemist at St Luke's Hospital, Guildford, Surrey, about the insulin injection upon Paul Crampton. Now Det Supt Stuart Clifton, in charge of the enquiry, knew that whoever was behind the deaths and ailments had access to restricted drugs within the hospital. But the police probe into the tragedies did not begin until 17 days after the attack on Paul Crampton – during which delay there was another murder and three more attacks. It was a lapse which has left many parents feeling bitter towards the authorities.

The police were able to draw certain conclusions in the case almost immediately. Every case had Allitt either treating the victim, or nearby when tragedy struck. She had access to proscribed drugs and in police questioning seemed sometimes over-eager to help police out in their enquiries. Her answers were plausible, but Det Supt Clifton said: 'As we collected more and more evidence we discovered that she had been lying. There was a dawning realisation on us that something had gone terribly

Above: ***Allitt en route to Grantham Magistrates Court. Parents who hoped for answers to what had happened to their loved ones were met with an arrogant silence.***

EVERY CASE HAD NURSE BEVERLY ALLITT EITHER TREATING THE VICTIM, OR NEARBY WHEN TRAGEDY STRUCK

THE Sun 25p

GROUP 4 CARTOON SPECIAL PAGE 3

Audited daily sale for April 4,081,624 (including Today)

Thursday, May 20, 1993 25p Today's TV: Pages 36 and 37

SCANDAL OF ALLITT'S JAIL LOVE

Love on the inside . . . kisses for evil Allitt

Sun EXCLUSIVE

Fury over gay fling

By MARTYN SHARPE and JOHN ASKILL

ANGEL of death Beverley Allitt is having a lesbian affair inside top security Rampton Hospital, it was revealed yesterday.

The 24-year-old nurse—awaiting sentence for murdering four tots on her ward—has confessed she is besotted with a "macho" arsonist called Sharon.

Parents of her victims were furious after hearing the pair had snatched moments of passion and been pictured kissing and cuddling.

Sue Phillips, whose nine-week-old daughter Becky was murdered by Allitt, said: "It's bloody disgusting that she's having a nice time in there while we're in pieces here.

"They should release her from Rampton, send her home to Grantham, and then the parents will deal with her. She wouldn't be having a nice time then."

Becky's twin sister, Katie, survived a poison attack by Allitt, and is now brain damaged. Chris Taylor, whose seven-week-old son Liam was murdered, said: "The families will never recover from losing their children, but now we're told Allitt's enjoying herself falling in love inside Rampton.

"All we ask is that she should suffer for what she's done.

"It's disgraceful that we hear about

Continued on Page 13

HERE COMES RENTA SONIC

Deal on games at £2 a night

By NEIL SYSON

TOY giant Sega is to rent out games like Sonic the Hedgehog through a national video chain store.

Kids will be charged £2 a night for computer games from Blockbuster Video's 800 shops.

It will allow children to test them at home before deciding whether it is worth forking out up to £65 a game.

Arch-rivals Nintendo could now feel forced to hit back with a similar scheme to make their own games available. The two companies corner the £700million-a-year British market and have been blasted over high prices.

The Consumers' Association claims games cost under £10 to make.

Sega has allowed smaller shops to rent out games for a year, but Blockbuster paid more than £300,000 to become the first national outlet.

A spokesman for the Sun Mega Guide said: "It's about time – we have been calling for months for this to happen."

Above: ***News of Allitt's warped love-life in jail was splashed on to the front pages of newspapers.***

amiss'. She was not the only suspect, however, as police had to quiz all nursing and other staff at the hospital. It was a process that took a dreadful emotional toll, leading one totally innocent nurse to kill herself – in lawmen's eyes, another victim of the vile Allitt. Her caring colleagues were haunted by the crimes – night sister Jean Saville, 49, to the point where she took her own life. Police said at her inquest that they were satisfied she had no involvement in the tragedies. A friend of hers said: 'Her feelings of isolation, shock and horror were all too much to bear. We were all under suspicion. We had been quizzed by police, sometimes for five hours at a time. As a result we all had to work longer hours to cover for each other. The stress built up'. During coffee breaks and ward rounds nurses gathered to discuss the crisis on Ward Four. Allitt was always close by, eager and ready to join in the discussion never betraying any of her bestial actions. Another nurse said: 'She was always in the thick of it. It seems unbelievable that the person working so hard in those desperate situations was the one who had caused them in the first place. She was very concerned about the children, it seemed, and she became close to several of the parents'.

It was finally to be good old-fashioned detective work which nailed Allitt. A dozen officers were formed into a squad on 1 May 1991 at Grantham Police Station with sole responsibility to probe the hospital deaths. As detectives searched tirelessly for a common link between the deaths and collapses, a chilling pattern emerged. The first was the obvious fact that no mishaps occurred when she was off duty. The second was a wide probe into the hospital's use of insulin. After the test results on the Crampton boy nineteen other cases were studied more closely. It became apparent that in many of them the insulin, and in some cases potassium chloride, had been injected without authorisation and in amounts that were too high. In each case they were linked to Nurse Allitt. The third factor was the disappearance of a book recording which patients had been allocated to which nurses – a book which was eventually found in her home. The fourth factor was the disappearance of pages from the report on Paul Crampton's condition – they had been torn out.

Finally she was confronted and charged with mass murderer – and she didn't bat an eyelid. Det Supt Clifton said: 'When she was charged she didn't appear to be surprised at all. I still don't know why she did it.'.

ONE TOTALLY INNOCENT NURSE KILLED HERSELF - IN LAWMEN'S EYES, ANOTHER VICTIM OF THE VILE ALLITT

Beverly Allitt was remanded in Rampton top security mental hospital during the months after her arrest before her trial in 1993 which lasted for three months. She lost six stones while on remand, suffering from the slimmer's disease anorexia nervosa, and was placed on a constant suicide watch. At her trial she became the focus of the most intense hatred to grip the British public since Myra Hindley's trial nearly three decades previously. She pleaded not guilty but the evidence stacked against her was enough to condemn her and in May 1993 was found guilty of the four murders, the attempted murders of Katie Phillips, Bradley Gibson and Paul Crampton, and attacks on Kayley Desmond, Yik Hung Chan, Christopher King, Patrick Elstone, Christopher Peasgood and Michael Davidson. Parents who had hoped for some word, some indication from Allitt about why she had committed the heinous crimes were left disappointed. She left court not saying a word about why the murders had been carried out. The judge in the case said there would be counselling available for the jurors who had listened to such a litany of horror during the testimony.

ANGUISHED VICTIMS

A week later, amid the frenzied cries of anguished victims, she stood in court again to be sentenced to four life terms in jail. Again, she said nothing before she was driven away to begin the rest of her miserable life behind the bars and walls of Broadmoor, Britain's most secure establishment for mentally ill criminals.

Mad or bad? That is the question that has confronted experts when trying to come to terms with horror perpetrated on the scale of Allitt or Angelo. Allitt, it was heard at her trial, once exploded: 'I am not competent, far from it. I am one of the bloody crappiest nurses out. I am the lowest of the low'. This self-depreciation, evident also in Angelo, is common among Munchausen syndrome sufferers. And yet Dr David Enoch, a specialist in rare psychiatric disorders at the Royal Liverpool Hospital, said that it is not madness that afflicts the sufferer. He says: 'She is not mad, she is psychotic. When you are psychotic you lose insight and delude yourself. You do not know what you are doing. Those who suffer from Munchausen's know that they are not really ill and have insight into their actions. In Allitt's case, she would have known what she was doing with the children'.

ALLITT BECAME THE FOCUS OF THE MOST INTENSE HATRED SINCE MYRA HINDLEY'S TRIAL THREE DECADES BEFORE

Brian Masters, who wrote an authoritative account of serial murderer Dennis Nielsen, said all of us have the potential within to kill. In people like Angelo and Allitt it is the destructive power which has gained control. 'It's there', he said, 'and we spend most of our lives keeping it at bay. Sometimes people don't succeed and sometimes they become serial killers'.

Such serious fault lines as existed in the personalities of Angelo and Allitt finally split asunder – and the innocents died to glorify what they perceive as their own, miserable lives.

Below: ***The grim edifice of Broadmoor, home to Beverly Allitt for the rest of her days.***

CECIL JACOBSON
The Sperminator

At his trial, Dr Cecil Jacobson claimed that 'I haven't slept with anyone but my wife in 30 years of marriage'. Yet he stood accused of fathering at least 70 children. He had abused his position at his fertility clinic to live out a mad dream of fatherhood.

Twisted medical minds have long nurtured the idea of becoming creators of life. From Dr Frankenstein of gothic-horror fantasy to the grim work undertaken by Dr Josef Mengele in the death camp of Auschwitz – where his mission was to create a race of blonde-blue eyed children for his beloved Fuehrer – the medical fraternity has often been tainted by evil geniuses who twisted the moral of their Hippocratic Oath to suit their own ends. But rarely in modern times has a medical practitioner actually had the opportunity to live out his fantasy in such a warped fashion as one Dr Cecil Jacobson – the man who will forever go down in criminal history as 'The Sperminator'.

Dr Jacobson has every chance to reflect upon his unique 'work' in furthering the human race – sadly for him, however, it may be remembrance of things past from behind the bars of a prison cell. In March 1992 he was found guilty on 52 counts of fraud and perjury – charges which blandly masked his real crime of fathering 70 children, perhaps more, with his sperm artificially inseminated into clients of his fertility clinic. Dr Jacobson's perverted quest to build what he hoped would be an intelligent race of children was finally thwarted after he had fooled medical authorities for years.

At the end of a three-week trial in Alexandria, Virginia, in which Jacobson was both pilloried as an unmerciful con man and saluted as a scientific pioneer who sought only to relieve the suffering of childless women, the verdict left the doctor reeling in an exhausted state of resignation. 'I was astounded I was found guilty on any of these counts', said Jacobson, 55, once a highly respected genetic researcher. He said he made many mistakes during his practice but claimed he was convicted for nothing more than 'trying to help these people' – these people being simple, trusting, childless people who wanted more than anything in the world to have babies. But Jean Blair, one of the numerous women who testified against Jacobson, summed it up for all decent human beings when she said the doctor knowingly put his victims through a living hell. 'He will never know the emotional roller-coaster we were on', said Blair, noting that she suffered seven bogus miscarriages under Jacobson's care. 'We mourned every one of those dead babies'. Prosecutors described Jacobson as a swindler who injected women with high concentrations of hormones so that tests would show they were pregnant when they were not – all so he could enhance his reputation as a successful baby doctor and

Above and Opposite: ***They called Dr Cecil Jacobson 'The Sperminator'. He had arrogantly breached every moral and ethical code of his calling by artificially inseminating women with his own semen.***

RARELY HAS A DOCTOR HAD THE OPPORTUNITY TO LIVE OUT HIS FANTASY IN SUCH A WARPED FASHION AS DR JACOBSON

JACOBSON USED HIS OWN SEMEN AND FREQUENTLY POCKETED $20 FROM PATIENTS, SAYING IT WAS FOR THE DONOR

charge patients for more office visits. They also said that he intentionally misread sonograms, outlining tiny fetuses where none existed - again so that he could string patients along. They said Jacobson led insemination patients to believe that he had an anonymous sperm donor programme and that they could choose certain characteristics for their new children. He used his own semen and frequently pocketed $20 cash from patients, saying the money was for the donor.

Jacobson's attorneys attempted to paint quite a different picture, a portrait of a scientist who helped women who had been abandoned by other doctors, either because they were fast approaching menopause or had physiological obstacles to conception. 'I knew my semen was safe', said Jacobson, 'because I haven't slept with anyone but my wife in 30 years of marriage'. They conceded, however, that he misread many test results and was probably better suited to a lab than a clinic. The defence attorneys said that, on occasion, Jacobson used his own sperm, but only because he feared that semen available from sperm banks might be tainted with HIV virus or other diseases. The result, they say, is that many patients who had been told they might never conceive now have healthy, happy children.

PLEA OF INNOCENCE

'We think this doctor is innocent, that he was a pioneer in his field', said James R. Tate, one of Jacobson's attorneys. 'He was so far ahead of his time that back at the time of civil cases several years previously he couldn't find much support. We'll have a lot of support this time'.

Right: ***The perverted 'Angel of Death' Dr Mengele, in South America. Were his experiments at the Nazis' death camps so different from Jacobson's?***

Opposite: ***'I have done nothing wrong' was Jacobson's cry until the end.***

Below: ***The end result of the Nazis' experiments to create 'perfect children': some of the victims who were deemed 'not fit to live'.***

The jury of eight women and four men struggled for 22 hours over four days to reach its decision, meticulously examining the case count by count. 'Some of us had over 400 pages of notes', said jury foreman Daniel Richard, who said he at first was convinced of Jacobson's innocence. 'We spent four days just reconstructing each patient's history. That's what took so long. It was a matter of complexity'.

Assistant US Attorney Randy Bellows, who worked on the case for more than two years with the help of postal inspectors and the FBI, was clearly pleased with the results. But Bellows focused his comments largely on the victims, whom he thanked for going 'through the difficult process of coming forward and testifying at trial . . . and reliving very difficult and sad moments in their lives'.

Bellows gave special credit to patients who now have children fathered by Jacobson and who risked public exposure 'to contribute to this search for the truth'.

The prosecution noted that the 11 parents testifying against Jacobson had 15 children ranging in age from four to 14, with more than half of them aged nine or older. Many of the children, he argued, were old enough to discover accidentally their true parentage simply by watching television or reading a newspaper.

Jacobson's attorneys charged the government with endangering the psychological welfare of Jacobson's former patients and violating Jacobson's promise to the parents that the donor programme would remain anonymous. 'It is also ironic that what the government seeks to conceal from these children is that their genetic heritage may, in fact, be superior to what they would otherwise have received', Tate said. 'The donor could have been a vagrant who carried the HIV virus and who sold his sperm to a "sperm bank" used by Dr. Jacobson'.

A LENGTHY AFFAIR

The 15-day trial alternated between wrenching accounts by past patients and plodding presentations by scientific experts, capping a case that began four years ago when more than 20 patients brought malpractice suits against Jacobson for leading them to believe they were pregnant when they were not. The women testi-

Above: ***The beginning of the end: Jacobson seen going to court in February 1992 to answer the charges laid against him.***

DESPITE THE SHOCKING EVIDENCE, AMERICAN LAW DOES NOT IN FACT FORBID DOCTORS TO IMPREGNATE THEIR PATIENTS

fied in civil depositions and at a hearing before the State Board of Medicine that Jacobson gave them hormone shots that triggered false pregnancy tests, used phoney sonograms to perpetuate the fraud, and then told them their foetuses were dead and would 'resorb"'into their bodies. But in November 1992 the case gained notoriety when prosecutors brought a massive indictment against Jacobson, charging the man born in the Mormon state of Utah with using his own semen to treat women who came to him for what they thought was an anonymous sperm donor programme. Prosecutors said their evidence showed that Jacobson may have fathered more than 70 children for patients treated at his now-defunct Reproductive Genetics Clinic. The allegation that provoked massive news coverage as far away as Brazil, France, Britain and Australia – and global indignation that people's basic rights had been so callously violated. That number was pushed even higher during Jacobson's own testimony in which he said he had used his sperm to impregnate some patients he saw at George Washington University Medical Center when he worked there from 1972 to 1976.

Despite the shocking evidence American law does not in fact forbid doctors to impregnate their patients, and Bellows was forced to rely on commonplace mail and wire fraud statutes to prosecute the bulk of his case. Throughout the trial, despite dozens of government witnesses, the question of why Jacobson would lead women to believe they were pregnant and why he would impregnate his own patients remained blurred – although from observers on the outside there were many theories. Bellows and Assistant US Attorney David G. Barger argued that

Jacobson did it for money, saying that if a woman thought she were pregnant she would return for more office visits and refer more patients to Jacobson. They said the donor programme also was for money, explaining that using his own sperm saved him the expense of creating a legitimate donor bank. Jacobson's Reproductive Genetics Center in Virginia thrived in the 1970s after he became the first doctor in the United States to perform amniocentesis, a method of detecting foetal defects. But as other doctors began to offer the procedure, Jacobson lost patients and income, Bellows said during the trial. Richard, the jury foreman said that he and fellow jurors were convinced that it was 'ridiculous' to believe Jacobson acted for money and that, if anything, Jacobson 'undercharged his prices'. Richard said he felt Jacobson impregnated patients out of sheer ego – an overwhelming desire to play the role of creator, a Jesus Christ figure in his own mind whereby he was making a race of intelligent children in his own image. Psychiatrist James Anderson, who examined the case in close detail, concurred, saying: 'It is obvious that neither fame nor money nor any perverted sexual lusts were behind what he was doing. He was getting his kicks from playing Mother Nature. He saw himself as some kind of superman, the father of the human race. And he got away with it for a long time. There are probably 70 of his offspring walking around in society – perhaps even more – and how do we know how many of them may have inherited his berserk view of life? What kind of problems will these children have in the future? Will it be the sins of the fathers visiting them? These are the most disturbing aspects of this entire sordid affair – the possibility that he has spawned nothing but deviants into society who may yet wreak misery on the parents who will lovingly and tenderly bring them up.

CHARACTER EXAMINATION

'Examining his character, I believe that he was dreadfully frightened of failure and longing to create something more permanent on this earth other than mortgage payments, a home for his family and an impressive work record. He wanted to be recognised as a great man, even if it was only ever to be savoured in his own mind'. Juror Ronald Mattingly also chalked up Jacobson's misdeeds to a stubborn refusal to accept failure. 'He couldn't stop – he was trying something that didn't work and when he realised it didn't work, he didn't stop', Mattingly said. Deborah Gregory, a key government witness who had three bogus pregnancies, believed money may have

Above: ***How many had he fathered? The Sperminator didn't know, but he disputed figures put forward by the prosecution.***

Above: ***The Sperminator finds support in his wife Joyce (left) and his father Cecil Snr as he arrives at court.***

played a small part in Jacobson's thinking, but added that he also might have been pursuing the glory he knew when he brought amniocentesis to America two decades ago. 'Research and science is his first love and I believe he saw a way to make money, but also saw a way to experiment with something that might bring fame as well as fortune. He was looking for a new amniocentesis to discover', she said. 'But I resented him taking my money and using me as his guinea pig', Gregory added. 'Don't use me as your experiment and add insult to injury by taking my money and lying to me while you're doing it'.

Because of the quirks in the law which did not specifically forbid the good doctor from using his own sperm, the authorities had to get him primarily on fraud and perjury raps. As a result, prosecutors had to push aside questions of medical ethics and tailor a white-collar mail fraud case to accommodate a host of allegations that were anything but conventional.

Jack H. Olender, one of Washington's most experienced malpractice lawyers, compared the U.S. attorney's strategy of using multi-purpose fraud statutes against Jacobson to the prosecutions of old-time gangsters. 'The great gangsters like Al Capone were prosecuted for tax fraud or wire fraud because they couldn't get them on anything else – even though the things they had done to earn the money were much worse', Olender said. In 30 years of practice, Olender can remember only one other case in which a doctor was criminally prosecuted – a case in which a surgeon performed partial abortions and patients had to return for additional treatments. 'It really takes something very bad to transcend civil law into criminal law – something really outrageous', he said.

For America, that really outrageous thing was personified by Dr. Cecil Jacobson.

Gripped by the possibility that dozens of Jacobson's genetic offspring were enrolled in Washington and Virginian schools, newspapers, television companies and Hollywood production companies deluged the usually sedate Alexandria courthouse

LIKE GANGSTER AL CAPONE, JACOBSON WAS CONVICTED OF A LESSER CRIME THAN THE PUBLIC BELIEVED HIM GUILTY OF with requests for information, documents and front-row seats during the trial. He was eventually found guilty of travel fraud, convicted of mail and wire fraud for lying to patients, using the US Postal Service to order supplies and collect bills and using telephones to discuss treatment. The six perjury counts were based on lies Jacobson told during civil actions against him several years ago.

A CRUEL LIAR

When the sentencing came down on Jacobson a month later, it came down with a vengeance. US District Judge James C. Cacheris said he 'cruelly lied to women at the most vital and traumatic point in their lives'. He sentenced him to five years in jail – although he could technically have given him a maximum term of 280 years inside – but added the rider that it must be served without the possibility of parole or early release. He also ordered Jacobson to pay $116,000 in fines – around £85,000 – saying he had 'not seen a case where there has been this degree of emotional anguish and psychological trauma'. Before sentencing, which came several weeks after Jacobson was found guilty, he repeated claims he made before and during his trial that he never intended to dupe his patients and that he had dedicated his life to helping couples desperate for children.

'I was totally unaware of the anger, anguish and hate I have caused – until these proceedings', Jacobson told Judge Cacheris. 'I ask for their forgiveness so that the healing process can start. But I helped a great deal of other people'. But Dr Richard

JUDGE CACHERIS SAID JACOBSON 'CRUELLY LIED TO WOMEN AT THE MOST VITAL AND TRAUMATIC POINT IN THEIR LIVES'

Below: ***Guilty! But Jacobson still finds time to explain himself to the media after his trial.***

Falk, head of the infertility programme at Columbia Hospital for Women in Washington, appeared for the prosecution and ridiculed the notion that Jacobson had done no harm by sowing his seed so energetically. Falk says that at most sperm banks it is standard practice to limit the number of times a donor is used to prevent the possibility of half-siblings unwittingly marrying someday, thus risking retardation and birth defects among their own offspring. To Falk, the suggestion that Jacobson had used his sperm to father so many children was shocking. 'That's unconscionable in and of itself – to have a bunch of families in one area whereby it's almost sure that there'll be several children in a school who are half-siblings', he testified. 'If I was a parent of one of those children I would move right away from the area'. Jacobson, who was released on bond pending his appeal, concluded: 'I did not wish to hurt these people. I wished to help'.

JACOBSON DEFENDED HIS ACTIONS BY PROTESTING 'I DID NOT WISH TO HURT THESE PEOPLE. I WISHED TO HELP'

Opposite: ***Jacobson talks to reporters while facing the prospect of numerous years in jail.***

Below: ***Jacobson's wife Joyce was one of the few people who stood by him during his trial.***

TEARFUL TESTIMONY

Fighting back tears, a woman who testified during the 12-day trial that Jacobson was the biological father of her daughter said the sentence was 'fair', but added that 'nothing ever will make up for the pain she and her husband suffered. The woman, one of 11 parents who testified under pseudonyms to conceal their own and their children's identities from the media glare, said that 'the satisfaction is he can't practise now. Nobody should ever have to go through this again'.

Daniel M. Clements, chairman of RESOLVE Inc., a non-profit advocacy group on infertility issues, said that Jacobson's case and the subsequent publicity, has caused infertile couples all across America to exercise more caution in choosing treatment and physicians. 'Jacobson is viewed for what he was, which is an aberrant practitioner', Clements said. Cramming the building's largest courtroom, a standing-room only crowd of victims, gawkers, Jacobson supporters and journalists sat in mesmerised silence as Cacheris pronounced sentence and brought the nationally celebrated case to a close.

Throughout the criminal case, Jacobson and his attorneys maintained that he was a pioneer whose fertility medicine was on the cutting edge.

LETTERS OF SUPPORT

'All he did was try to help people', said James R. Tate, his attorney, noting that the judge received 90 letters of support from Jacobson's friends and former patients. 'This is breaking his heart. But he still has his integrity and stood up for what he believed in'. Cecil Jacobson Sr., the doctor's father, denounced the case as a government 'witch hunt' and denigrated those who complained about his son as gold diggers who saw an opportunity to make money through civil suits. 'This has not broken our family apart. It's brought us together', said Jacobson's father. 'This thing is all going to blow apart at some point'. Joyce Jacobson, the doctor's wife, said she was insulted by the suggestion that he was greedy for cash. 'We don't buy fancy clothes, and you should see the cars we drive', she said. She also suggested that her husband's use of his own semen was an obvious and safe alternative to expensive donor banks. 'It's like giving blood to me – what's the difference? It has shock value, but when you think about it, where are you going to get better sperm?' The family also took some pleasure in the fact that Cacheris rejected the government's request to have Jacobson jailed while he pursues his appeal, a process that prosecutors estimated would take a year. Assistant U.S. Attorney Randy I. Bellows, who had asked the court to put Jacobson behind bars for ten years and make him pay more than $1 million in

fines, nonetheless expressed satisfaction with the five-year term, noting that it is a harsh sentence for a white-collar fraud case. Bellows said that Cacheris's ruling made it clear that 'when a doctor is found guilty of lying to his patients on matters of fundamental importance, there will be a severe sentence meted out'. On Tate's request, Cacheris said he would ask that Jacobson be allowed to serve his time at the minimum-security federal prison at Nellis Air Force Base in Las Vegas. The prison, where inmates live in dormitory-style rooms without bars and may be allowed to work on the base, is one of the closest to Jacobson's Utah home. Cacheris ordered that $39,205 of the $116,000 fine be used to compensate witnesses who testified that they had been wronged by Jacobson and who had not collected money through previous civil suits.

THE EFFECT THAT JACOBSON HAD ON THEIR LIVES IS STILL TOO MUCH FOR SOME WOMEN TO COMPREHEND

What he did is still too much for some women to comprehend. Carole Franda, another former patient, has a 13-year-old son as a result of insemination at his clinic. Because of his notoriety now she says; 'There is this shadow and cloud over the paternity of these children. This is tearing families apart. It's hurt the grandparents. Most couples never told their parents about the insemination. You have grandparents who loved and doted on these children'.

MORAL DILEMMAS

At the time of writing, The Sperminator is still free while the legal process grinds inexorably onwards towards a verdict. But whatever his fate, it is left to the parents who relied on him to decide what to tell their own children. For Carole Franda, who presumed she was being impregnated with her own husband's sperm, the choice has been made to keep herself – and him – in the dark. 'I love him for what he is', she said. 'If I had his DNA tested he would know that I was questioning his paternity. The fact is he is a human being I love and I think other families should adopt this frame of mind too'.

Below: ***How Britain's* Daily Express *reported a scandal that touched a nerve in every parent.***

Guilty! The Sperminator

Doctor who artificially inseminated women himself faces 280 years in jail

THE BABYMAKER: Jacobson leaving court with wife Joyce yesterday

From IAN MacGREGOR in New York

A FERTILITY doctor was last night found guilty of secretly using his own sperm to make his patients pregnant.

Self-styled "babymaker" Dr Cecil Jacobson fathered up to 75 children.

The 55-year-old specialist pretended he was using anonymous sperm donors.

But he was caught out when some mothers noticed their children looked like the chubby doctor.

One woman testified that she noticed her daughter's resemblance to Jacobson in a photograph when the baby was just three days old.

Another patient said he told her: "God doesn't give you babies — I do."

Jacobson now faces a jail sentence of up to 280 years and about £300,000 in fines. But he showed no emotion when the verdict was read out.

Doctors are not forbidden from using their own sperm, but Jacobson's patients were told the sperm was from medical students.

They were able to choose characteristics like eye colour, religion, and hair colour.

Yet a former lab technician for Jacobson said there was no sperm bank and the doctor often went into a bathroom to fill vials.

Lying

Jury foreman Daniel Richard said outside the court: "We knew he was lying to those patients."

Jacobson, who has seven children by his wife, Joyce, always said he did not hurt anyone.

"I've never knowingly lied to a patient," he claimed. "I have misinformed out of ignorance."

The jury in Alexandria, Virginia, found him gu[...] of 52 counts of fraud [...] perjury.

He was also accuse[...] tricking women [...] believing they were p[...]nant when they were [...]

Jacobson said last ni[...] "I spent my life tryin[...] help women have [...]dren. It is a shock t[...] found guilty of tryin[...] help people.

"I certainly did not [...]fully or intentionally h[...] anyone."

But prosecutor Ra[...] Bellows told the court [...] doctor was a "man [...] routinely lies to his [...] patients."

Jacobson admitted o[...]sionally using his [...] sperm when donors [...] not available.

But he claimed he [...] not know how many [...]dren he fathered.

He will be sentence[...] May 8.